ARTS AND CRAFTS STYLE AND SPIRIT

CRAFTSPEOPLE OF THE REVIVAL

ARTS and CRAFTS STYLE and SPIRIT

Chase Reynolds Ewald

GIBBS·SMITH
P
PUBLISHER

Salt Lake City

For my mother, who recently discovered her own Arts & Crafts heritage.

First Edition
02 01 00 99 5 4 3 2 1

Text copyright © 1999 by Chase Reynolds Ewald
Photograph copyrights as noted throughout.

Published by Gibbs Smith, Publisher
P.O. Box 667
Layton, Utah 84041
Visit our Web site: www.gibbs-smith.com
Order toll free: (1-800) 748-5439

Cover design by Traci O'Very Covey
Interior design by Kristin Bernhisel-Osborn

Jacket photographs:
Center front: column clock by Jim Dailey with pot by Jerome Venneman; photo by Ryan Drew Mellon
Back: tiles by Motawi Tileworks
Back: detail of chair by David Hellman

Facing the title page: Gamble House art-glass door, photo by Chase Reynolds Ewald

Printed and bound in China

Library of Congress Cataloging-in-Publication Data
Ewald, Chase Reynolds, 1963–
Arts and crafts style and spirit: craftspeople of the revival / Chase Reynolds Ewald. — 1st ed.
p. cm.
ISBN 0-87905-894-3
1. Handicraft—United States. 2. Artisans—United States. 3. Arts and crafts movement—United States. I. Title.
TT23.E93 1999
745.5'092'273—DC2
98-45262
CIP

CONTENTS

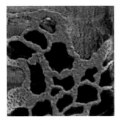

ACKNOWLEDGMENTS

It was a special house that ultimately led to this book; thus, I'd like to acknowledge architect Henry Herold, a fellow of Taliesin West, who designed our home in the style of his mentor, Frank Lloyd Wright.

I owe a debt to Amy Eliot, architect and friend, on whose advice I first visited the Craftsman's Guild and discovered the world of contemporary Arts & Crafts.

For their input, advice, and introductions, thanks to Barbara Klein and Andrea Leal at the Craftsman's Guild; Lee Jester at Craftsman Home; Lee Sanders at the Gamble House; Robert Melita and Peter Smorto at Peter-Roberts Antiques; Colleen McGlynn; and author Ralph Kylloe and his wife and partner Michelle.

A very special thanks is due Bruce Smith and Yoshiko Yamamoto for their help, advice, contacts, photographic images, and just plain friendliness, without which this book would be less than it is. I cannot thank them enough.

The contemporary craftspeople featured herein all gave generously of their limited time; I am as appreciative of that as I am in awe of their work.

I have the greatest respect and appreciation for my agent, Diana Finch. Madge Baird is a veteran editor—diligent, unflappable, and kind. Thanks to her and to all the folks at Gibbs Smith, Publisher, for their professionalism.

For fine meals and various roofs overhead while traveling to research this book, I'd like to thank my parents, Russ and Debbie Reynolds, Janet Davidson and Richard Platt, Tom Ewald, Dick and Bitsy Hotaling, and Bo and Anna Polk.

On the home front, "Obrigada!" to Marivone, Flor, Magda, and Ione, who helped free me up to write this book; to Addie, Jessie, and Ross, who cooperated fully when not providing much-needed distraction; and, always, to Charles—for everything.

Leading Arts & Crafts workshops of the day often collaborated on furniture and fixtures such as this lamp, with its leaded-glass "vine border" lampshade from Tiffany Studios combined with a ceramic and electrodeposit copper base by Kataro Shirayamadani for Rookwood Pottery, circa 1901.

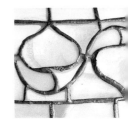

Art is the flower, life is the green leaf. Let every artist strive to make his flower a beautiful living thing, something that will convince the world that there may be—there are—things more precious, more lasting, than life.

—Charles Rennie Mackintosh

The Arts & Crafts movement professed to be about ideas and ideals, society and social mores. Fundamentally, however, like any movement, it was ultimately about people. The individuals who gave shape to this marriage of style and philosophy—and thus transformed the way people lived, and thought about living, both abroad and in the States—were characters whose personalities still flourish today through their writings, designs, and idealism.

John Ruskin's socially conscious essays and William Morris's manifestation of ideals into handworked reality, coupled with the forward-looking artistic genius of such designers as Charles Rennie Mackintosh, C. F. A. Voysey, and C. R. Ashbee, generated an international Arts & Crafts movement that rose up and drew breath, then crossed the Atlantic on the wings of philosophical ideals and a body of functional craft.

While the Arts & Crafts movement transformed the way Americans approached the concept of home, Americans transformed the movement into something uniquely American. True to the melting-pot concept of a basis for a new society, the American movement borrowed freely from the European Arts & Crafts movement as well as ancient design motifs of Asia and architectural elements of its own indigenous cultures. It made liberal use, without apology, of the very processes of mechanization whose dehumanizing influence on workers gave rise to the movement in the first place. Nowhere was it more fully embodied than in the figure of Elbert Hubbard, the movement's most flamboyant proselytizer, whose lectures, publications, and artisan community in upstate New York attracted millions—yet whose goal nevertheless was to build a business.

Today's American Arts & Crafts movement has plenty of colorful characters, but its flamboyant proselytizers are few. Whether one terms it a revival or merely the continuation of a stylistic movement that lay dormant for several decades, Arts & Crafts today is made up of a surprisingly close-knit and enduringly warm community of artists and craftspeople, scholars and writers, antiques dealers and collectors, and bungalow dwellers.

Like their forebears, today's craftspeople offer an antidote to contemporary societal concerns. They address matters about the environment by using sustainably grown woods and selecting materials with a heightened ecological consciousness; to counteract the effects of a "throwaway" society, they build furniture and fixtures designed to last for hundreds of years. They overcome the loss of community by creating guilds and participating in a nationwide Arts & Crafts network in supportive, sharing roles. They counter the homogenization of society and the cheapening of contemporary products by crafting unique designs that celebrate the past while looking to the future.

Facing
The Arts & Crafts movement began in England as early as the mid-1800s with the writings of John Ruskin and Augustus Pugin. Ideals took practical form at a later time through the works of William Morris and others. Early furniture designs, such as these Ford Maddox Brown-designed bedroom pieces, were simple and even somewhat austere in line.

Photograph courtesy the Grove Park Inn.

hand-hammered copper hardware and lamps hearken back to medieval times; pottery glazes reflect the deep, rich, subdued hues of nature; textiles offer a tactile experience through pinpoints of color in nature-derived motifs on textured natural linen; the straightforward functionality of a Morris chair or Stickley-style chest of drawers allows the subtle beauty of quartersawn oak to serve as its own ornamentation; Greene & Greene-style tables point to their joinery with pride; Prairie School spindle-backed chairs speak of line and form, beauty in utility.

The craftspeople featured herein are representative, but by no means inclusive, of the best in contemporary Arts & Crafts design; there are scores more artisans working singly and in groups scattered from New England to southern California and all points in between. They draw from the design vocabularies of the movement's European founders—as well as the Stickley brothers, the Roycroft artisans, Frank Lloyd Wright, Dirk van Erp, Charles and Henry Greene, and turn-of-the-century ceramicists, to name just a few—and use them as a springboard for their own creative artistry. Their work is in the style and the spirit of the movement's original designers, yet it is wholly their own.

These craftspeople aren't Luddites, by any means—they take advantage of machinery and computers, after all—but in each case the emphasis is on handwork. The resulting furniture, lamps, vases, pillows, and glasswork have a timeless quality with craftsmanship evident upon first glance and simple elegance that will hold its own stylistically over centuries.

At the Grove Park Inn of Asheville, North Carolina, site of the country's premier Arts & Crafts conference, collectors say that the movement never died. As these pages will attest, the movement continues to evolve— right into the next millennium.

Above
For close to a century, Grove Park Inn guests have enjoyed sweeping views of the surrounding Blue Ridge Mountains from the inn's terrace. Original furnishings included works from Roycroft, Stickley, and these Old Hickory rockers.

Facing
A major Arts & Crafts resort still in business today (and the site of the country's premier Arts & Crafts conference, show, and sale), the Grove Park Inn, in Asheville, North Carolina, was an ultimate expression of Organic Architecture. Built in 1913 of huge, locally quarried granite boulders, the hotel is furnished with furniture from the workshops of Stickley, Limbert, and Roycroft.

Now going on thirty years, the Arts & Crafts Revival may be described as a nostalgic urge to fight the effects of contemporary society by curling up in a Morris chair by the fireplace with a good book. But that would neglect the fundamental appeal of a style the movement spawned: simple yet sophisticated, evocative yet timeless. Because of this, the furnishings, particularly contemporary interpretations, are equally at home in a classic bungalow surrounded by Arts & Crafts antiques, a rustic lakeside lodge, or a New York loft apartment decorated with modern art.

Stylistically, the movement is both a revival and an evolution—which is immediately apparent in looking at the work of today's scores of Arts & Crafts artisans scattered across the country. In furniture, in metalwork, in art glass and mica, in textiles and ceramics, the Arts & Crafts Revival celebrates the vision of the movement's founders while bringing it securely into the twenty-first century.

Craftspeople making straight reproductions are few, but in all the work featured in this volume, the founders' approach to design is evident. As it was a hundred years ago,

Gustav Stickley's log home at Craftsman Farms, constructed in 1910 in Parsippany, New Jersey, was a showplace for his espousal of the simple life. It was Stickley (1858–1942) who was responsible for popularizing the term "Mission," and for sending the message into the homes of thousands through *The Craftsman.*

The living room of Stickley's 5,000-square-foot home on the twenty-six-acre Craftsman Farms featured log walls, warm woodwork, a stone fireplace with a copper hood, and—of course—Stickley furniture. The building (recently restored and open to the public) was originally intended to be a meeting hall for the craftsmen Stickley hoped would visit from other countries.

"There are two kinds of people to be found in all studios," wrote Elbert Hubbard, "those who talk about art and the fellows who paint the pictures."

The craftspeople featured here *do* talk and know about the Arts & Crafts movement. They are as familiar with their forebears as though they knew them personally, they are well-read, and the literature on their work is often sprinkled with quotes from John Ruskin, William Morris, Gustav Stickley, and Elbert Hubbard. They enjoy seeing each other's work and being part of a flourishing contemporary Arts & Crafts community. But most of all they are workers. They don't have business hours, and their vacations are often related to their vocations. In each case, their work is their life, literally.

John Ruskin, the philosophical founder of the Arts & Crafts movement, said, "The workman ought often to be thinking, and the thinker often to be working."

The artisans of the Arts & Crafts Revival are thoughtful workers; they are working thinkers.

Photograph ©Linda Svendsen.

Ford Maddox Brown's designs from the late 1850s—like this stained green settle reproduced by Roger Moss and Audel Davis from the collection at Kelmscott Manor, William Morris's country estate—were intended for working people. Simplicity, utility, solidity, and honesty were their characteristics.

It is no accident that there has been a renewed appreciation for the simple lines and harmonious effect of the Arts & Crafts style a full century after the term was coined.

Then, as now, there was an uneasy sensation that the world was hurtling into the future on fast-forward, that much was beyond our control. A hundred years ago that feeling was provoked by sweeping changes: the mass movement of society from farm to city, the stunningly rapid technological advances with manufacturing mechanization, and the advent of electricity, automobiles, and the telephone. The original Arts & Crafts movement as conceived in the 1870s and 1880s, hit its full stride from 1895 to 1920, and faded into the design annals of obscurity in the face of cataclysmic world events and changing tastes.

On a macro level, the Arts & Crafts movement was an effort to save society through art. On a micro level, it offered a welcome respite from the oppression of a Victorian living room. In reality, the movement was a stylistic approach to living that fit the realities of modern life while offering a refuge from the sometimes horrific changes going on outside the door.

Almost exactly one hundred years later, stimulated by a 1972 exhibit curated by Robert Judson Clark at Princeton University, Arts & Crafts came out of the attic. It has since gained vigor and momentum, spawning not only a lucrative antiques trade and a renewed appreciation for the forward-looking, philosophically based design geniuses of the time, but also a new generation of

artists, craftspeople, and thinkers who comprise today's Arts & Crafts Revival.

Now, as then, humanity needs an antidote for the rapid technological and widespread societal changes it faces. In Arts & Crafts—both in style and philosophy—home offers the ultimate refuge.

■ Origins

Philosophically and aesthetically, the Arts & Crafts movement was conceived in England. As early as the mid-1800s, British Reformers John Ruskin and Augustus Pugin were decrying the changes transforming modern civilization from a rural, agrarian, community-based society to one that was industrialized, mechanized and urban-oriented. The production line, they asserted, took dignity away from the worker and exerted a dehumanizing influence under which individuality was squelched, conformity ruled, and mediocrity flourished. The urban squalor resulting from the processes of industrialization—teeming streets, open sewage, coal smog, disease, dangerous working conditions—gave rise to the importance of home as a place for retreat and renewal. In the breakdown of close-knit multigenerational communities, the need for home as the center of moral character development became truly urgent.

Ideals aside, stylistically the movement was a reaction against the excess embellishment and increasingly shoddy construction techniques of the Victorian age at its height. Enough of the heavy drawing rooms filled with knick-knacks; elaborately carved and overstuffed

Pasadena architects Charles and Henry Greene created the ultimate expression of holistic design in their homes and furnishings, bringing to bear all their artistic excellence and understanding of craftsmanship. At first strongly influenced by Stickley's heavy, solid oak pieces, their furniture styles evolved to feature intricate joinery, Asian influences, inlays of rare woods and mother-of-pearl, and beautiful finishes. From . leaded glass and lighting fixtures to chairs, beds, and entire buildings, they exhibited a mastery of proportion and scale, and pushed wood to its fullest possible potential, as evidenced in the dining room of the 1909 Thorsen House in Berkeley, California.

The actual implementation of the ideals espoused by Ruskin and Pugin is credited to William Morris, a prominent English designer, poet, author, and critic. He gave practical application to their ideas by setting up a company that trained workers in ancient handcrafts, elevated craft to the level of art, and made beautiful designs on quality goods available to the public, albeit the upper-middle-class public. His company created designs for home embroidery as well, thus laying the groundwork for an aspect of the Arts & Crafts movement that remains important to this day: the availability of the healthful and moral benefits of craftsmanship to anyone. His efforts also spurred an interest in art needlework to the extent that schools and institutes offering craft training sprang up throughout the country, bringing craftsmanship into the lives of the vast middle class. The victims of the industrial revolution—the poor, the displaced, the downtrodden—were also given the opportunity to enrich their lives and station through craft with the establishment of such centers as Toynbee Hall, founded in 1888 by reformers in a London tenement neighborhood and imitated by Chicago's Hull House, founded soon after in 1889.

It was Morris who said, in 1882, "Have nothing in your house that you do not know to be useful or believe to be beautiful," a phrase oft-quoted today. His designs, like his writings, are still vibrant after more than one hundred years. They are adapted for utility: textiles, wallpapers, and stained-glass windows. And they are indeed beautiful, featuring rich, repeating patterns derived from the garden.

■ Across the Atlantic

The tenets of the movement migrated across the Atlantic even before the term Arts & Crafts was in wide use. Exhibitions at the

A Charles Limbert oval lamp table, built in 1907, and Stickley chair were classics of the movement.

furniture; walls covered with artwork; ornate, massive frames; intricately patterned rugs and wallpaper; heavy drapes that barred the uplifting effects of sunlight and fresh air! The effect was pretentious, not to mention oppressive. People were ready for rooms in which they could breathe.

Wall treatments such as this mural brought nature into the Arts & Crafts home.

Right

A 1904 lady's writing desk by Harvey Ellis for Stickley is a study in utilitarian beauty. Under the Mackintosh-influenced Ellis, who Stickley originally hired in 1903 to work on designs for *The Craftsman*, Stickley furniture became more refined and sophisticated.

Photograph courtesy the Craftsman's Guild and California Heritage Gallery.

Below

An ideal Arts & Crafts living room, shown here in a 1905 issue of *The Craftsman*, offered clean lines and a homey warmth through its wood surfaces, rectilinear furniture, muted colors, and natural linens.

Philadelphia Centennial Exposition in 1876, such as that of the Royal Society of Art Needlework, gave rise to the formation of the early crafts societies in the States.

The Society of Decorative Arts was founded in New York City in 1877 by Candace Wheeler (who later went on to oversee textile production at Louis Tiffany's design firm). The Society offered classes and exhibitions; soon similarly intentioned organizations were springing up all over the country. For instance, Newcomb College, which was established in New Orleans in 1895, taught pottery and needlework, both to empower regular people to bring the joy of handcrafting into their own lives and, on a more practical level, to train women in skills that could translate into paying jobs.

Although the term *Arts & Crafts* wasn't formally used until it appeared in an announcement by the English Arts & Crafts Exhibition Society in 1888, its precepts were already established. As soon as the term was coined, however, Arts & Crafts societies—the Chalk and Chisel Club in Minneapolis, 1895; the Guild of Arts & Crafts in San Francisco, 1896; the Chicago Arts & Crafts Society, 1897; and the Rochester Arts & Crafts Society, 1897—sprang up in its wake.

■ A Holistic Approach

In the following decades, the movement grew on both sides of the ocean and saw the American version's most prominent characters traveling to Europe and coming home inspired. The Europeans visited the United States, too, and a synergy developed: there were, in Scotland, architect and designer Charles Rennie Mackintosh and the Glasgow School; in Austria, the Vienna Secessionists such as Josef Hoffman; in England, architect/designer C. F. A. Voysey and C. R. Ashbee; and in the United States, architects

Frank Lloyd Wright in Chicago, Bernard Maybeck in the San Francisco Bay Area, Irving Gill in San Diego, and Charles and Henry Greene in Pasadena. The result was an espousal of the unified complete environment. From the outside in, from landscaping to home furnishings, the movement's figureheads preached a holistic, wholesome, all-inclusive approach to home life.

Architecture and landscaping were intended to fit in and reflect the countryside in which they lay. In America, where homes were being built at a great pace for the growing middle class, structures were generally small and intimate and designed to open up to the outside in windows, generous sheltered porches, and, where regionally appropriate, sleeping porches. Floor plans were more open, reflecting the belief that families should come together rather than retiring to compartments, the designs were more efficient, too—an important consideration with the disappearance of the household servant.

The architectural vocabulary drew on international styles suited for the locale. When possible, designs incorporated locally abundant materials—redwood in California, adobe in the Southwest, for instance—displaying a nascent environmental consciousness. The architecture of the Prairie School was characterized by long, low horizontal lines that reflected the vast plains of the Midwest. The bungalow, which reached its full expression in southern California, was boxy and compact, made of natural materials, and featured sheltering eaves, broad porches, and a single level to maximize household efficiency. Rustic buildings like the great camps of the Adirondacks and the grand lodges of the West's national parks featured rough bark and burled wood that brought nature inside, with soaring spaces mimicking the mountains and lakes. These structures represented the

Photograph courtesy the Craftsman's Guild and California Heritage Gallery.

ultimate expression of "organic architecture," in which buildings would appear to grow out of their sites.

The holistic approach meant that the furnishings were as important as the structure. The leading architects designed not just buildings but furniture, lighting, textiles, tableware—

The signature inlay work of Harvey Ellis (1852–1904)—a major influence in Arts & Crafts design whose artistry still inspires many today—is showcased in this rocker.

The figurehead of the Chicago-based Prairie School and one of the greatest design geniuses of the twentieth century, Frank Lloyd Wright was fascinated with the horizontal line and with geometric shapes, as evidenced in the dining room of the 1908 Boynton House in Rochester, New York.

The Swedenborgian Church, built in 1894–95, with its open-gabled ceiling supported by unpeeled madrone tree trunks, its rush-seated chairs in place of pews, and its large masonry fireplace, was and is a picture of rustic simplicity in the heart of San Francisco.

even, reportedly, in the case of Frank Lloyd Wright, a dress for the lady of the house.

■ Approach to Craft

Outside and inside the home, the byword was honesty: honest materials, honest construction.

Furniture was of an appropriate material—usually good solid American oak—cut to reveal the grain and for maximum strength, and fastened together with joinery using such techniques as through-mortise-and-tenon, which was seen as both honest and a sign of solid, enduring craftsmanship. Metalwork showed the mark of the craftsman's hammer, while copper and bronze (and, though not frequently used, semiprecious stones) were favored over gold, silver, and precious jewels as more accessible to the populace. Hardware was heavy, almost medieval in appearance, with a hand-forged look.

Draperies were made of light, natural fabric, with nature-derived handwork for decoration, replacing the heavy curtains that screened the inhabitants of Victorian homes from nature. Pottery and tile were rendered

in earthen hues and classic forms and were finished with satiny matte glazes; any embellishment drew from the flora and fauna of the surrounding countryside. Art glass was very popular. Wright's designs were almost musical, tending to play with shape, motif, and repeating colors, while in the stained glass of William Morris, Louis Tiffany, and John La Farge, color and design were allowed to find full expression. The graphic arts flourished too, in bookbinding, papermaking, and printmaking.

Despite the hearkening back to medieval times in straightforward, almost austere, unembellished form—such as Stickley's Mission furniture—the furnishings could be very forward-looking in design, with a decidedly modern feeling. Charles Rennie Mackintosh's and Frank Lloyd Wright's impossibly tall, narrow-backed, rectilinear chairs must have astounded Victorian sensibilities when they were introduced; indeed, they still look modern today.

■ Regional Expressions

As the movement spread across the country and was embraced by a growing number of people—largely thanks to Gustav Stickley's *The Craftsman*, Elbert Hubbard's *The Philistine* and *The Fra*, and leading women's magazines of the day, such as *House Beautiful* and *Ladies' Home Journal*—different approaches flourished in various regions of the country. All, however, espoused simplicity.

The largest concentration of Arts & Crafts in the East was in upstate New York, and its greatest influence was exerted by Elbert Hubbard and the Roycroft "campus" in East Aurora. Founded as a bookbindery in 1895 and later gaining renown for its copperwork and furniture-making, the semi-cooperative (but profit-oriented) venture and the exuberant personality of Hubbard, with his flowing locks and penchant for philosophizing,

Photograph courtesy the Craftsman's Guild and California Heritage Gallery.

drew visitors—and converts to Arts & Crafts—in droves. During its height in the early 1900s, Roycroft boasted 300 employees; three monthly publications, one of which had a circulation of over 100,000; and, in one month alone, 28,000 visitors.

Charles Rohlfs in Buffalo and Gustav Stickley in Syracuse produced furniture for the masses, with Stickley responsible for popularizing the term "Mission." He sent the message into the homes of thousands through *The Craftsman* magazine (first published in 1901), with its emphasis on bringing craft into the home. It was Stickley who popularized the bungalow, selling both the plans and the furniture to go in it. He also strongly advocated the beneficial effects of craft for all individuals, encouraging

hobbyist craftsmen through the sale of kits and plans. New York was also the home of Arts & Crafts community Byrdcliff, founded in 1902. Nearby in Pennsylvania was Rose Valley, founded in 1901.

Boston was a hot spot, too. A center for bookbinding and printing, it was also the home of Grueby Faience. Founded in 1894, it was one of the many American potteries that made Europe sit up and take notice at the 1900 Exposition Universalle in Paris.

In the Midwest, the Prairie School, whose figurehead was Frank Lloyd Wright, was characterized by horizontal lines, open floor plans, lots of windows (often in unexpected places like the corners of rooms), natural

Arts & Crafts design—featuring sturdy construction, natural wood, exposed joinery, straight lines, and minimal embellishment—was all the rage by 1905, when Charles P. Limbert (1824–1923) built this sideboard. The rocker and club chair are also from Limbert.

site-appropriate materials, a central hearth, geometric and nature-inspired stylized designs, and built-in cabinetry and seating. Wright would build 119 buildings in ten years during the height of the Prairie School period; for the 1902 Dana-Thomas House alone, he created almost 100 furniture designs. And Wright was only one of twenty architects associated with the Prairie School.

Other creative outlets sprang up throughout the heartland, most notably Charles Limbert Company (1902), another Mission-furniture manufacturer, and Gustav Stickley's brothers, Leopold and J. G. Stickley (1900) in Michigan. Moravian Pottery in Pennsylvania, Pewabic Tile in Detroit, and Rookwood Pottery in Cincinnati showcased naturalistic motifs and unique signature glazes. In founding Rookwood on the cusp of the Arts & Crafts movement in 1880, Maria Longworth Nichols created an entire movement in Ohio, home to thirty potteries at one time.

On the West Coast, the San Francisco Bay Area was a hive of activity for Arts & Crafts proponents, especially after a 1906 fire destroyed much of the city. Here architecture and metalwork in particular flourished, although there were a number of noted ceramics works, too. Bernard Maybeck's Swedenborgian Church in San Francisco, with an interior that was Shaker-like in its simplicity and dependent on massive trusses for the soaring ceiling, still stands as the ultimate expression of organic architecture in an urban setting. The metalwork of Dirk van Erp—both in its craftsmanship and design—is still the standard by which hand-hammered copper is measured today.

The Arts & Crafts movement coincided with a population boom in southern California—the fabled promised land with its undeveloped land, pristine beaches, and vast orange groves. It was a place to which the bungalow

The Gamble House, built by Charles and Henry Greene in 1909 in Pasadena (now owned by the University of Southern California and open to the public), was a revelation in craftsmanship in all details from design to joinery. It inspires countless craftsmen still.

Photograph courtesy of the Minneapolis Institute of Art.

Architect George Grant Elmslie, for many years Louis Sullivan's chief draftsman, and his partner William Gray Purcell were well-known Minneapolis-based members of the Prairie School who also designed furniture. While their work bore a resemblance to that of their more famous peer Frank Lloyd Wright, their signature touch is evident here in the repeating block motif found between the spindles.

design, developed in Britain's colonial outposts, was ideally suited, and in which elements of Spanish and Mission design could be adapted in honor of the region's rich cultural heritage. Sleeping porches and over-hanging bungalow rooftops, used liberally in the architecture of Charles and Henry Greene, were ideal for the temperate climate, as were the nature-inspired tiles produced by Ernest Batchelder. In San Diego, Irving Gill's flat-roofed, modernized pueblo homes reflected the movement's interest in indigenous architecture.

The Greenes created the ultimate expression of holistic design in their homes and furnishings, bringing all their artistic excellence and

understanding of craftsmanship to bear on their creations. With master artisans Peter and John Hall, they turned out 400 pieces of furniture between 1907 and 1915. At first strongly influenced by Stickley's heavy, solid oak pieces, their style evolved to feature intricate joinery, Asian influences, inlays of rare woods and mother-of-pearl, and beautiful finishes. From leaded glass (by master artisan Emil Lange) and lighting fixtures to chairs, beds, and entire buildings, they exhibited a mastery of proportion and scale and pushed wood to its fullest possible potential.

Ironically, the English movement, so firmly based on idealism and elevating the less privileged, rejected the use of machines, thus

San Francisco Bay Area metal-worker Dirk van Erp (1859–1933), a Dutch immigrant, made a lasting contribution to Arts & Crafts design in his works of hand-hammered copper.

Photograph © Timothy Hansen, courtesy Roger Moss.

Photograph courtesy of Fulper Pottery.

■ Decline and Revival

It wasn't just the death of Elbert Hubbard on the *Lusitania* in 1915 that led to the rapid decline—and virtual disappearance—of the Arts & Crafts movement. Society was moving forward, thrust into World War I, followed by the Great Depression and World War II. When the populace was revitalized enough to consider matters of style, it was to seek a fresh, contemporary outlook that would lead it into the next era of prosperity.

Both the furnishings and the ideals of the Arts & Crafts movement were relegated to the attic for several decades; even major museums sold their collections as irrelevant—folk art, at best. It was the 1972 Princeton exhibition that sparked the realization that Arts & Crafts style is just as relevant today as it was a century ago. The exhibition was followed by a rapid and increasing embracing of the style, resulting in a renewed appreciation for turn-of-the-century Arts & Crafts companies still in operation today, such as Pewabic and Moravian tileworks, and Judson Stained Glass Studios, and also those that have been revived, such as Stickley Furniture and Fulper Tile.

The subsequent popularity among celebrities of Arts & Crafts antiques in the eighties served to enhance their stature and fuel their desirability—and increase their value. Many of today's prominent Arts & Crafts artisans, in fact, came to their craft through an appreciation of the style and its underlying

Ceramics—tile and pottery—were an important aspect of the original Arts & Crafts movement, as they are in today's Revival. Ceramics helped bring affordable handcrafted items into the home, but they also provided an opportunity for individuals to learn a craft, thereby ennobling their own lives through creative handwork—an essential tenet of the original movement's philosophy. In 1909, William Hill Fulper II introduced a line of pottery that earned him "Master Craftsman" status with the Boston Society of Arts & Crafts; by 1915, Fulper Pottery was on exhibit at the Panama-Pacific Exposition. Seventy years later, Fulper Pottery was revived by four of the founder's granddaughters, who discovered the pottery's secret glaze formulas stashed in an attic.

producing items affordable only to the more wealthy. Except in the case of the Greenes and Frank Lloyd Wright, whose work generally only the affluent could afford, American proponents embraced the use of machines. Thus, while still advocating handwork, they were able to offer quality furniture, lighting, and other goods to vast numbers.

philosophy, coupled with the reality that original works had become too expensive to buy:
if they wanted Arts & Crafts harmony in
their lives, they would have to make clocks,
furniture, pottery, or lighting themselves. In
the case of textiles, the originals generally
weren't in good enough condition to tolerate
daily use as intended. Other craftsmen
already working as artisans were drawn to
the style through the honest, sturdy warmth
of Stickley furniture, the design genius of
Frank Lloyd Wright, or the artistic vision,
coupled with technical mastery, inherent in
the works of Charles and Henry Greene.

The Arts & Crafts movement has come full
circle in a hundred-year evolution. It has
become mainstream again, and runs the range
from the highest-priced antiques to museum-
quality reproductions and original
contemporary designs to mass-produced furnishings featured in nationally marketed
catalogs and major shelter magazines. Artisan
guilds are springing up around the country as
well, promoting the philosophy of craft raised
to the level of art.

Whether one calls it a revival or a natural
evolution of an enduring style, the romantic
longing for the past inherent in Arts & Crafts
style has been translated into fresh, contemporary designs in the hands of today's
artisans. Using the original movement's
designs as a creative springboard for artistic
excellence, the works celebrate the joy of nos-
talgia and a style fit for a new millennium.

Photograph courtesy of the Minneapolis Institute of Art.

The Purcell-Cutts House, built in
1913 in Minneapolis, now owned
by the Minneapolis Institute of Art
and open to the public, featured
horizontal lines and leaded-glass
windows. The furniture in its guest
bedroom was designed by
the architects and reproduced
by contemporary craftsman
Michael McGlynn.

David Berman
*English Arts & Crafts
Fixtures and Furniture*

It's a common story in the Arts & Crafts world: someone moves into an Arts & Crafts home and, in a subsequent voyage of discovery, becomes obsessed by the movement. That's David Berman's story but with a twist.

Nineteen eighty-two was a transition year for Berman. He had made a business out of restoring old houses around New England, but a newfound allergy to the pesticides used in his work forced him to stop. "My next love was furniture," he says. Fate found him both a workshop and living space in a Massachusetts house called Trustworth, "an amazing place built in 1889 that really did look like Sleeping Beauty's castle." He would remain twelve years.

Berman's interest was in making reproductions of nineteenth-century American furniture, and this he started to do. In the meantime, though, the building—a major Arts & Crafts-period house built in 1889—and Henry Turner Bailey, its longtime owner who had died in 1931, started to work their influence.

"Henry Turner Bailey was one of the leading art educators in Boston," Berman explains. "Before 1917 he was responsible for art education in the state of Massachusetts. From 1917 to 1930 he was the dean of art at the Cleveland Art Institute. He was the editor of *School Arts Magazine*. He'd been the American liaison for the International Art Congress in London at the turn of the century. Every summer he would take groups on art tours, to Florence, Venice, all through Europe, and England.

"The studio was closed in 1931, and his archives were totally intact when I arrived in 1982. The archives were in an amazing room that had 150 pasteboard boxes of his files, with additional file cabinets built into the walls. He subscribed to all the magazines, plus all his files and notebooks were there. I could read his diaries and know exactly what he was talking about and what he was doing at a particular time. He was an architect as well, and his drawing table was there, his sketches. . . . As for the house, the books were all still in the same place; all the furniture was still the same as when he lived there. Henry Turner Bailey was a great person to have as a teacher—even though he died in 1931."

The American Arts & Crafts movement reached its full expression during Bailey's career, with the majority of Americans having become aware of Arts & Crafts and Mission furniture through mass marketing. Bailey's attention, however, was fixed on England, specifically on the work of Charles Francis Annesley Voysey, an influential English architect of the 1890s and 1900s who also designed furniture.

Voysey's finely crafted yet simple wooden chairs and beds showed lines not dissimilar to the later American Mission furniture (although usually without the massive feel). Despite tapered legs and rounded arms, they were sturdy and straightforward with an inherent, understated elegance. "Voysey felt that furniture should be left unornamented and that the sophistication should come from its geometry and proportion," Berman

Above right
Exquisite designs and meticulous craftsmanship, the Greenes' legacy, is carried on by James Ipekjian in his inlay work, here of oak, rosewood, and mother-of-pearl. Photograph courtesy the artist.

Facing
David Berman's career as a craftsman began with his fascination with the work of Charles Francis Annesley Voysey, an influential English architect and furniture designer of the 1890s and 1900s. Berman's reproduction of a Voysey clock is elaborately hand painted and inscribed.

Photograph © Scott Dorrance.

Artisan David Berman's second career as a restorer of homes was put to good use in the restoration of the building that became Sconehenge, the bed-and-breakfast Berman runs on Cape Cod.

explains. "For instance, an upright on a chair leg will often start as a square, then taper to an octagon. Something can seem comparatively simple yet really be an advanced study in geometry."

Voysey's clocks and barometers were more whimsical, bearing handpainted designs that often incorporated birds and pithy sayings. ("Time and tide wait for no man" is inscribed over a background of trees, sailboats, birds, and flowers on the first piece Berman reproduced, a clock for his brother's wedding gift.) What Berman found particularly enchanting were Voysey's flat designs, which he adapted for lighting. (Voysey's own lighting designs were "somewhat primitive," according to Berman.) Wood and metal frames provide the setting for intricate metal cutouts through which the light shines; motifs are naturalistic, with birds being a favorite subject. Voysey's designs for wallpaper and textiles were on par with those of William Morris, again usually incorporating stylized designs from nature.

Berman also reproduces works of other English designers of the same era. For instance, his case pieces after E. W. Godwin and William Burges are large-scale and elaborate. Painted and stenciled, they bear impressive hand-wrought hardware.

As a result of his research, David Berman became obsessed with the Arts & Crafts movement, but like his mentor, he too was looking East across the Atlantic. "It's really what made me into an Arts & Crafts craftsman. While I was making seventeenth-, eighteenth-, and nineteenth-century American furniture reproductions, I was starting to absorb the archives—and it was fascinating. Because of Bailey's clipping files and his interest in Voysey, I became very interested and started to reproduce Voysey pieces just for my own enjoyment. Then I started to get a little press."

Soon Berman had not only built a reputation for his English-inspired work, but had become an acknowledged expert on Voysey and the English Arts & Crafts movement. The fact that Voysey designed one-of-a-kind pieces for specific houses presented an unusual situation: on the one hand, the designer wasn't that well known, particularly not in the U.S. in the 1980s. On the other hand, Voysey's works were virtually unavailable, creating an opportunity for a craftsman to work with that limited but highly discerning group of collectors who might be interested in Voysey's work.

"All his pieces are in museums—or lost," Berman says. "If someone sees a piece in a book, there's usually only that one. I work with people who are either rounding out their collections or have a particular interest in English Arts & Crafts. My clients know exactly what they want."

Now, he says, "there's perhaps more appreciation for Voysey here than in England, although Voysey-designed houses are being used in films such as *Shadowlands* and *The French Lieutenant's Woman* to create a mindset, an atmosphere."

Berman spends a lot of time in England, but most of his clients are Americans. One of them, however, just purchased a Voysey house in London, and Berman will be responsible for all the movable furniture in the house. "It's great to be putting furniture in a Voysey house," he enthuses. "I'm thrilled to death to finally get a chance to work on a real one."

Berman does make furniture, but his primary focus is on lighting fixtures, clocks, and barometers. He has designed fabrics and wallpapers that are produced in conjunction with J. R. Burrows and is working on a line of Voysey-inspired carpets. His Trustworth Studio offers a line of needlepoint kits from Voysey patterns on handpainted canvas. An English major in college, this craftsman is completely self-taught—except, of course, for what he learned from Henry Turner Bailey.

Berman has never lost interest in American houses, however. Despite the allergies, he just had to do one last project: a dilapidated house in Plymouth, which he bought, restored, and turned into "Sconehenge," a thriving bed-and-breakfast just minutes from the Cape Cod Canal. The rooms are filled with fine workmanship and plenty of Voysey influence.

His studio-workshop, an open, sunlit space, is on the third floor, but it might as well be a century—and a continent—away.

Todd Brotherton
Fine Furniture in the Arts & Crafts Tradition

Todd Brotherton was having a bad time. The major piece he was working on—an eight-foot-long sideboard influenced by Frank Lloyd Wright's case work—was past its delivery date and there was no end in sight.

A series of mishaps he couldn't have imagined and was barely able to endure kept setting him back every time he felt he was making progress. In one memorable three-month period, he sent the piece to the finisher and

Photograph courtesy the artist.

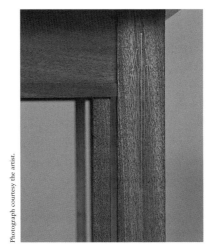

Photograph courtesy the artist.

Above
Todd Brotherton's mahogany table, after a writing desk by Harvey Ellis, features ebony details and pewter inlay.

Left
Brotherton completed the inlay work for this table by pouring the pewter as liquid, "just to see if it could be done."

immediately afterwards found evidence of wood-boring beetles in his workshop. Not knowing whether the piece could have been affected, he felt the only thing to do to ensure its integrity was to pick it up from the finisher, have the sideboard fumigated in a safe place, and have his own workshop fumigated. This all took some time, which, of

Furniture maker Todd Brotherton started fine woodworking as a luthier; the attention to detail demanded by that craft translates well to the work of Frank Lloyd Wright and Greene & Greene.

Photograph © 1999 Chase Reynolds Ewald.

course, caused him to lose his place in line with the finisher.

Finally the piece was finished. Brotherton went to pick it up and it was beautiful. Then he noticed, in anguish, that there was an almost imperceptible "cupping," a warp to the top of the sideboard. Probably no one would even notice it except him. Nevertheless, there was only one way to go from here: take it home, remove the top, make it perfect again, and repeat the process.

"It happens sometimes," he says simply. "That's the nature of wood. It's a living thing; it wasn't created in a factory. There can be unseen stresses that are part of the wood. Things happen that are sometimes difficult to control. But that's the nature of woodworking, to learn how to work with these elements. Sometimes it's a real challenge. But there can be fun in that, too."

By now the finisher couldn't fit him in at all; so, Brotherton delivered the piece to his back-up finisher several hours away. He waited a

couple of weeks and called the finisher. The phone rang and rang. He dialed for days in a row, and there was never an answer. He called a friend in the area and asked him to go to the place to see what he could find out. The friend reported that the shop appeared to have been closed down by the fire department.

Well, the story goes on and includes health problems, El Nino's snowstorms, and a variety of other complications. By now Brotherton knew he would never begin to be paid for the time he had put into this piece. "The circumstances were extraordinary. I'd never had anything happen like this. A lot of people would have shoved it out the door [before it was perfect], but I couldn't do that. You're either motivated by the love of the work or motivated by money. For me, it's about making the piece the best it can be."

Brotherton came to woodworking, oddly enough, through a love of music. A lifelong Californian who grew up with a handyman father and woodworker grandfather, Brotherton had always loved music and musical instruments, and studied music from the age of ten. "It was my first love in life," he says. When he and his wife moved to Mount Shasta in northern California in 1974, he started making instruments. "I had purchased a guitar built in 1930 but was dissatisfied with some of the repair work that had been done on it. I bought a book on working with guitars, then just started working on inexpensive instruments I'd pick up at garage sales. That was my introduction to woodworking."

Brotherton was making his living as a mechanic at that time, having learned from his father. But two years after moving to the country, Brotherton's career as a mechanic ended abruptly when he was badly burned in a gas explosion. By then, his instrument-making experience revealed his innate passion for woodworking. He got a contractor's license,

focusing mainly on high-end interior work, namely, cabinetry. Over the next couple of years, he recalls, he moved more and more into higher-end woodworking.

"I guess my sensibilities were set with instrument-making," Brotherton says. "I really like refined work, I like working with hand tools. I have as much machinery as anyone, but I'm not much of a machinist. I would much rather spend the time doing it by hand."

Brotherton has been crafting furniture since 1978. His work has been heavily influenced by the Arts & Crafts movement in general and Greene & Greene in particular since 1983. Like the Greenes, he looks to the East for inspiration. "My own aesthetic always ran along Asian lines," he says.

Brotherton is largely self-taught, although he did have a mentor, an artist/sculptor/woodworker friend, who "always shared his

knowledge and thoughts willingly. He taught me how to approach design along both objective and subjective avenues. He taught me to separate those things. It was real important in helping me say what impact a change in design would have."

This proved especially useful in two recent projects: a contemporary rustic table for a home in New York, in which not one piece except the top is straight; and a table patterned after a writing desk by Harvey Ellis. Made of Honduran mahogany, the table features ebony pegs and legs with pewter inlay running down their sides. "This is traditionally done by forming the pieces first, but this was poured as liquid pewter. It was quite difficult," Brotherton says, in characteristic understatement. "The lines are an eighth of an inch wide; if the pewter is too hot, it burns the wood, and if it's too cold, it balls up like mercury does. I just wanted to see if it could

Inspired by Frank Lloyd Wright's casework designs, Brotherton built an eight-foot-long sideboard made of 600-year-old quartersawn white oak and fitted with brass hardware.

be done." Other recent projects include a Stickley-inspired wardrobe, a side chair after the Greene brothers' Robinson House dining chairs, and a Greene & Greene-inspired blanket chest with silver and ebony inlay.

The best part for Brotherton is working with wood. He reveres wood. He buys it only from specialty sawyers scattered around the country. "The pieces are usually from old trees and come in two- to three-foot widths. In old wood—because of the temperatures it's endured, the forests it grew in—you get a quality and texture that is wonderful. The wood in the sideboard, for instance, came from a 600-year-old oak tree in Virginia. I love working with this kind of wood that comes from old trees that have finally died. I feel like I'm giving it a second life and creating an opportunity for others to see what that wood is like, what it can be. In doing so, I feel I'm sharing my values, my belief in the importance of having things that last in a throwaway society. I'm selling part of myself in the pieces I create."

Brotherton's clients find him mostly by word of mouth, although he does place advertisements in magazines from time to time. "People come to me when they can't find what they're looking for in the stores. They come to me when they want something more than just a piece of furniture. They want a piece with . . . ," he pauses, "life, is one way to put it."

Jim Dailey
Clocks

Moving from an Arts & Crafts bungalow in Pasadena to a farmhouse surrounded by fields on an island in rural Washington State may seem like a major transition, but clock maker Jim Dailey is able to carry the Pasadena Arts & Crafts influence inside him while letting his craft find full expression in its current rural setting.

Photograph © Ryan Drew Mellon.

Like most natives of Pasadena, Dailey would have been hard-pressed to grow up knowing nothing about the Arts & Crafts movement. It wasn't until he bought a run-down 1912 bungalow in a deteriorated neighborhood on the edge of the old downtown area of Los Angeles, however, that he fully discovered the style and philosophy that had such a grip on the region at the time his house was constructed. It may have been the late 1980s, but he was living in the teens.

"When we saw this beat-up old Craftsman on a hill," Dailey recalls of his and his partner Vince's compulsion to buy the house, "we just had to have it." A painter by training with an M.F.A. from Claremont Graduate School, Dailey was in the middle of a ten-year stint as an art teacher at nearby Antelope Valley College. Woodworking had already become an important means of self-expression by then, although he was mostly self-taught. "I had a cousin who taught me how to use a table saw when I was fourteen. I'd always liked to make things."

Photograph © Ryan Drew Mellon.

Facing

Jim Dailey turned his hobby into a vocation when he sold his first Arts & Crafts clock at the Gamble House Bookstore.

Jim Dailey's craftsman clocks are equally at home in an Arts & Crafts bungalow or a turn-of-the-century farmhouse.

Dailey and his partner had taken on the restoration of an old farmhouse previously. The do-it-yourself aspect of fixing up a home had appealed to them, as did getting out of the rent-paying cycle and the possibility that their neighborhood lay in the path of L.A.'s gentrification process. It was when they had "brought the house up to a nice level," Dailey recalls, that they discovered and bought the bungalow.

As often happens, the home started exerting its influence on them immediately. "I'd recognized the Arts & Crafts style as a teenager when my brother brought home a Stickley-esque chair he'd bought at a garage sale for fifteen dollars. In the mid-'80s I bought my first Stickley rocker at a swap meet for $100. We started collecting Craftsman furniture, and soon I was lusting after a Stickley mantel clock. At several thousand dollars, or whatever they were going for then, I couldn't afford one, so I decided to make one."

Dailey sent away for a clock-making kit and was on his way. "The faces were pretty ordinary, though. I used a traditional Arabic numeral face on the first one and was disappointed. Vince does computer graphics and suggested we scan some old fonts. He started printing the faces, then we ended up silkscreening them. That's when I felt I had a product that was unique."

At the time, Dailey was volunteering as a docent at the Gamble House, the Pasadena masterpiece of Charles and Henry Greene. It wasn't long before one of his clocks was offered for sale in the gift shop there. The sale of that first clock in 1991 emboldened him to quit his teaching job in 1992.

In 1993, they moved to Washington, to a turn-of-the-century farmhouse on Fir Island. Dailey works in a converted horse barn on the property. With an entourage of cats and dogs to keep him company on his short commute, a prolific garden to tend in the summer months, and plenty of wood scraps to burn in the shop's woodstove in the winter, Dailey is living the Arts & Crafts ideal: a simple, good life in a beautiful, nature-oriented place with meaningful work.

Like Arts & Crafts practitioners of old, the artisan often feels caught between the philosophy that insists handmade work should be affordable to all, and the reality that the handmade work takes so long to produce and requires such a high level of craftsmanship that it is almost impossible to make a living if one offers competitive prices. It is certainly impossible to compete with more-mass-produced items offered in catalogs and from production-oriented workshops. "I try to keep the prices affordable to the common man. I may be failing in that regard," Dailey adds, "since I often feel I'm not making any money."

Living in the country helps, as does the fact that there is not a lot of competition in clock making. And Dailey offers variety with eight basic models, six clock faces, and endless variations. From the "Arroyo Pendulum," adapted from a Stickley design first published in *The Craftsman* magazine, and an appealingly straightforward Mission design inspired by Harvey Ellis, to more contemporary "Prairie" and "Buffalo" styles of his own design, boredom is never a problem—and Dailey never finds himself wondering how to spend his time.

David B. Hellman
Greene & Greene-Inspired Furniture

Passionate is a word craftsman colleagues use when describing David B. Hellman's enthusiasm for the work of California architects and designers Charles Sumner Greene and Henry Mather Greene. It becomes clear upon talking to Hellman, even briefly, that crafting furniture worthy of the Greenes' artistic genius is the driving force in his life.

Hellman has recently completed a hall table, a scaled-down version of one the Greenes designed for the entry of the Gamble House, their Pasadena masterpiece. Made of mahogany, with hand-carved drawer pulls, the table features a cloud-lift motif on its upper rails and numerous ebony details that add grace and elegance, all combining to convey an overall serenity. Perhaps most interesting are the striking finger joints on the drawers. They were left "proud" and punctuated with ebony pegs; suspended lightly from ebony hangers, they remain visible even when the drawers are not extended.

"This table is incredibly smart in that it's extremely functional," enthuses the artist. "The long overhanging top with the small base means it does not take up a lot of floor space, yet it's very stable because the legs get thicker at the bottom. It has incredible detail, but it's not only decorative—it's structural. It has lots of storage in the drawers because the drawers hang off the top, yet it doesn't need a big base to carry them. The wood will darken

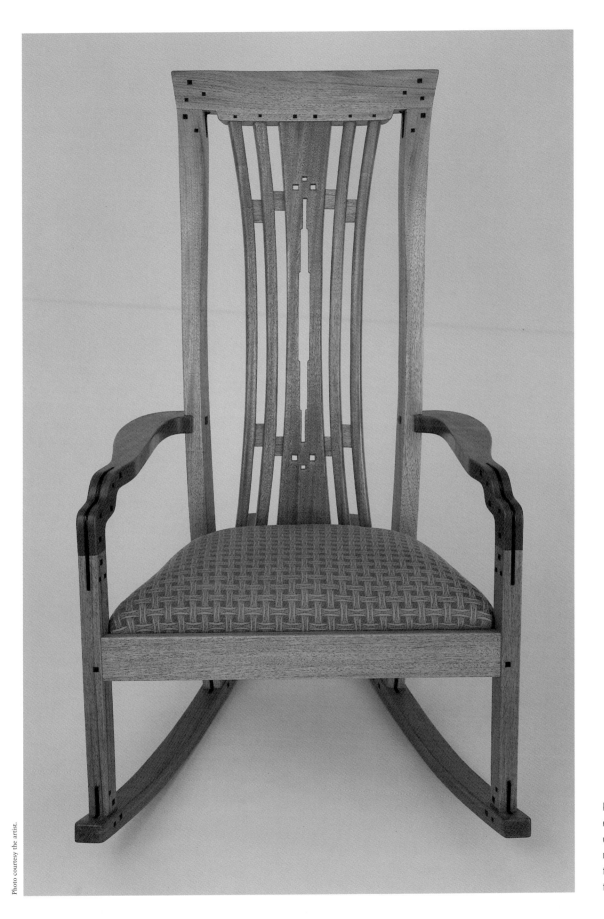

David Hellman's signature piece developed over the course of a decade: a rocking chair of mahogany and ebony based on the living-room armchair built for the Blacker House in Pasadena.

Massachusetts furniture maker David Hellman feels the touch of Greene & Greene from across the continent.

Photograph courtesy the artist.

David Hellman's mahogany table, a scaled-down version of the hall table the Greenes designed for the entry of the Gamble House, has hand-carved drawer pulls, the cloud-lift motif on its upper rails, ebony details, and, on the drawers, striking finger joints, which are left proud and punctuated with ebony pegs.

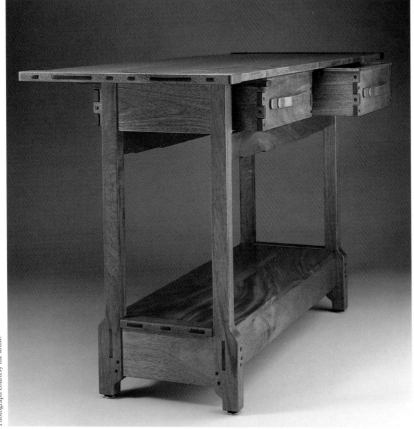

Photograph courtesy the artist.

over time with oxidation and will just get better with age. The finger joints, each one proud like that, and the way each corner is rounded over and softened, there's no quick way to do that. The Greenes did that to make a statement.

"This design is timeless," he concludes. "And this is just *one* piece in *one* home, yet it's typical of their work. And their houses," he continues, "the Gamble House, the Thorsen, the Pratt—they're houses that are built like pieces of furniture. You just couldn't do that today. And when you see them up close, you see the craftsmanship, the design. . . ."

He says, finally, "I consider the designs of Greene & Greene the ultimate expression of the American Arts & Crafts movement. Their furniture was executed at the highest level by the most skilled craftsmen at the peak of their careers. Their attention to detail in both furniture and architecture is unparalleled. *That* is what drives me to attain the same high level of accomplished cabinetmaking."

Hellman has been interested in building furniture for as long as he can remember. By the time he was an undergraduate at the University of Southern California, he was spending all his spare time in the wood shop of the architecture school. "I couldn't wait to get over there," he recalls. Furniture making as a career, however, seemed neither feasible nor practical for the psychology major. "I took it all the way to the other extreme," he says. "I got licensed as an eye doctor."

The graduate program took him to Boston, where he met his future wife, who worked at the New England School of Optometry. Despite the rigorous academic schedule, he still made time for some weekend woodworking classes. Still, the detour into professional life took eight years. "I became a professional test taker, then had a successful practice and employees. Then I decided life's too short. You should do what you really want to do. Of course," he admits, "it took a lot of time to make this decision."

In 1989 Hellman enrolled in the North Bennett Street School in Boston, graduating in 1991. A school with a hundred-year history, its original mission was to train new immigrants in the trades; it has now become a haven for adults in mid-career transitions, teaching such esoteric trades as bookbinding, cabinetmaking, preservation carpentry, violin making, and piano technology. In furniture, he says, "the school was more traditionally based—Chippendale, Queen Anne, Federal styles. I did do a practice ball-and-claw once, but it went against my grain."

One instructor, however, was interested in the work of Greene & Greene, which Hellman, despite his southern California upbringing, hadn't known much about. When Hellman was at work on a Greene & Greene-inspired rocking chair, the two flew out to Pasadena to see some of the original work up close. "My heart was racing the whole time. You just know when you've found your life's work."

Hellman has worked alone and done everything himself, right down to the finish. Now, though, with a year's backlog of orders, he's expanded and taken on an assistant. Despite his reverence for the masters of the ultimate bungalow, he does consider other projects. A recent work is a scaled-down replica of the massive tall-case oak Roycroft clock that graces the great room of the Grove Park Inn. In this, too, he is attentive to all details. He went through a number of copper workers before settling on one who knew how to make the patina take on the appearance of leather, who could handle repoussé work on the Roman numerals instead of soldering them on, who could achieve the effect Hellman sought in the mammoth strap hinges.

Photograph courtesy the artist.

After that, though, it's back to the Greenes, specifically, a dining-room table based on one designed for the Richardson House, with chairs based on preliminary sketches for the Thorsen House.

As for the Roycroft side trip, he says, "This is a very special project. I wasn't going to say no. And I'll learn a lot. But my love—my passion—is Greene & Greene."

For a wholly original Arts & Crafts rotating book table, Hellman combined cherry, a maple burl top, blood wood, and brass inlay.

James Ipekjian
Greene & Greene Reproductions

James Ipekjian has come a long way from the Philadelphia-style highboy he built for his dentist as his first commission nearly thirty years ago. Although he subsequently built in traditional French, English, and Art Nouveau styles, these days his name is virtually synonymous with Greene & Greene.

Known for his painstaking reproductions of Greene & Greene furniture and lighting since the mid-1980s, Ipekjian was intimately involved in the restoration of the Greenes' Duncan-Irwin House in Pasadena back in the early eighties. More recently he acted as master craftsman and woodwork consultant for the restoration of the Blacker House, the Greenes' masterpiece bungalow in Pasadena, for which he also built lighting and furniture. His work resides in the Gamble House (outdoor woodwork and a reproduction of a living-room table the Gambles chose to keep when they donated the house to the University of Southern California), and the Huntington Library's permanent exhibition of the Greenes' reconstructed Robinson House dining room. (There the doors, wall cabinets, sconces, and wood trim are by Ipekjian). His work can also be seen in such non-Greene & Greene Arts & Crafts icons as the living room of Frank Lloyd Wright's Hollyhock House in Los Angeles.

Having been born and raised in the master architects and furniture designers' hometown of Pasadena, proximity surely played a role in his evolution from self-taught hobbyist woodworker to Greene & Greene master artisan. However, as a youth, he wasn't aware of the now-famous brothers.

"From the middle of their careers, their popularity waned as tastes changed," Ipekjian points out. "People were looking to the modern movement or the Spanish Revival. It was

Pasadena artisan James Ipekjian—here with a pair of wardrobes in white oak bearing a floral motif based on a Mackintosh design—is an expert on Greene & Greene through his restoration and reproduction work.

when the Gamble House became public in 1975 that people could experience it. The Gamble House is probably the single most important reason for the renewed interest in Arts & Crafts in southern California.

"At the time I was starting out I'd had experience with Greene & Greene in that I had seen their work and had been to the Gamble House. From my perspective, just seeing their work in books or exhibitions and seeing the incredible level of craft certainly whets your appetite. At that time there was really no other place to go see their work except the Gamble House. Other houses that had originally had furniture in them were no longer furnished with the original pieces. So I knew it existed and I appreciated it, but I didn't actively pursue trying to build in that style. However, in the early 1980s a friend bought the Duncan-Irwin House; this was a person I had met by chance, a doctor interested in woodworking. One day he said, 'Let's go look at a house I'm considering buying.' It was in atrocious condition, but he bought it and did a remarkable job restoring it.

"I really cut my teeth on Greene & Greene," he recalls. "When the Duncan-Irwin House came along, in order to do it, I had to learn. In this recent era of appreciation of the Greenes' work, the Duncan-Irwin House was the first house to undergo a major restoration, and it was a learning process for everyone involved. The first order of business was to get the place cleaned up—strip paint, etc.—which was not what I did. But I would make suggestions; I was sort of a consultant on the wood. I made the light fixtures, cabinetry, rebuilt the courtyard benches and mantel, made a dining set, many tables, and a number of chairs. The list goes on and on. It was a lot of fun.

"The work I did there was seen and appreciated by a few people, so I was given the opportunity to bid on re-creating the lighting for the Blacker House. On a daily basis there were issues that came up in the Blacker House where, because of my earlier work, it

Ipekjian's painstaking reproduction work includes the living-room furniture for Frank Lloyd Wright's Hollyhock House in Los Angeles: couches with attached writing desks and torchères bearing the stylized hollyhock motif Wright used throughout the house.

Photograph © Tim Street-Porter

Photograph © 1999 Chase Reynolds Ewald.

Photograph courtesy the artist.

Ipekjian is well known for his highly crafted Greene & Greene reproductions, such as this mahogany sideboard patterned after that of the Thorsen House in Berkeley.

An Asian sensibility infuses the work of Greene & Greene—and of Jim Ipekjian, who built this reproduction of the Charles Greene-designed gate of the Gamble House in Pasadena.

was natural for me to get involved. I ended up being a kind of technical expert on wood—which was everything. It didn't start off that way, but I don't think anyone at the beginning understood what it was going to take. It became like peeling an artichoke, trying to get to the heart of it and finding one layer after another. To their credit, fairly early on the owners decided not to live with something that was second best."

Ipekjian is gratified by the results of the long hours and head-scratching that went into the two restorations. Not only are the Duncan-Irwin and Blacker Houses restored to their former glory, but the research and work done on each contributed significantly to the body of knowledge of the Greenes' work. "A lot of processes had to be developed during the Blacker House restoration, mostly through trial and error," he says. Now, though, the

same knowledge is being applied to work being done on the Greenes' Freeman-Ford House as well as Charles Greene's own home, both in Pasadena.

Of Ipekjian's relationship with the Greenes' work, he says, it was an evolution—and perhaps, fate. "It didn't happen overnight. And it shouldn't have."

From his early days as a woodworking hobbyist (while employed as a model-maker in the aerospace industry), he built from photographs, books, common sense, and instinct. As a consequence of never having been formally instructed, he says, he's not a very good teacher and tends to work best alone. "It's somewhat of a downfall for me now," he concedes. "Plus, I tend to be a little impatient. I have a standard to which I work: it has to look a certain way; it has to feel a certain way. My standard has evolved from what I've been exposed to. If the work master craftsmen Peter and John Hall did for the Greenes hadn't been as good as it was, I probably wouldn't have been drawn to it."

Ipekjian has been so involved with restoration and reproduction work that he hasn't had much opportunity to allow his own creative instincts full freedom to roam. He did receive a commission several years ago to build some dining-room pieces for a house in Pasadena. "They said, 'We have a space and want cabinetry; you design it.' It was about the first time that opportunity presented itself, and it was great."

Inevitably, the resulting sideboard and leaded-glass display cabinets showed the Greenes' influence. "I don't know what would happen if I just sat down to design," muses the crafts-man. "I've been so enmeshed in Greene & Greene for so long that it would be difficult for it not to come out somehow."

Sue Mack and Kevin Rodel
Furniture Inspired by the Glasgow and Prairie Schools

Sue Mack and Kevin Rodel have a lot in common. They're both from Philadelphia; both discovered a love of woodworking as young adults despite having no real exposure to it; both committed to an Arts & Crafts aesthetic in their work more than a decade ago; both love music, especially traditional and Celtic; both yearned for the community experience of small-town life even though they came from city backgrounds. Of course, they're both married—to each other.

It has been a journey of discovery since the day they met in a music store in Philadelphia (they both played five-string banjos) in the seventies. Although Rodel had done some woodworking growing up, he was mostly self-taught through woodworking magazines at that point. A social worker who hated the pay, the working conditions, and the bureau-cracy, he dreamed about becoming a woodworker. Sue Mack had always been interested in woodworking, too, but the doors of her high-school wood shop were firmly closed to women.

"Girls were never exposed to woodworking," she says. "I took home economics and typing and filing—all those things girls were

Photograph © Dennis Griggs.

expected to learn. But I'm six foot two; I knew I was a different kind of person. When I met Kevin we realized we both liked wood-working. We didn't really know what it was," she laughs, "but we knew we liked it."

Charles Rennie Mackintosh (in the grid pattern on the lower shelf) meets Harvey Ellis (in the inlay work) in Mack & Rodel's Glasgow Coffee Table.

Woodworkers Sue Mack and Kevin Rodel, of Mack & Rodel, comprise the best-known husband-and-wife partnership of the Arts & Crafts Revival. Their work is inspired by designers of the Prairie and Glasgow schools, as well as Greene & Greene, Charles Limbert, and Harvey Ellis.

Photograph © Dennis Griggs.

They both enrolled in nighttime woodworking classes, while Sue took a new job at the Franklin Institute, a science and technology museum. There she started hanging around the wood shop on her lunch break. The two resident craftsmen, who made the exhibits for the museum's shows, ". . . liked me, they took to me, they let me watch." When one left, Mack petitioned for his job. "I had to be forceful," she recalls of the bias against women in woodworking shops, "but I got the job."

In the meantime, Rodel was accumulating his own shop experience as a volunteer on tall ships. Old wooden boats, of course, ". . . always needed something done, like repairing doors and rotting fixtures." Mack and Rodel started sailing on the ships as deckhand and engineer respectively, and, on one of the longer cruises, discovered Maine. "We had heard there was a lot of opportunity for woodworking, both places to learn and places to work," Rodel recalls. They moved

Mack & Rodel's Argyll Hunt Board is the successful result of a collaboration between client and craftsmen. This piece showcases antique tiles from the client's collection.

Photograph © Dennis Griggs.

Photograph © Dennis Griggs.

Above
Mack & Rodel use some Arts & Crafts motifs—through tenon, art glass, and square cutouts—in their highly original Brög Bench.

Left
Mack & Rodel's distinctive Brög (Gaelic for "shoe") Bench was designed for use as a dressing bench, with a lower-than-average seat and drawers underneath. A nine-square grid at both ends adds visual interest with stained-glass inserts that catch the light.

to Maine in 1978 and married shortly afterwards. After a brief just-pay-the-bills-experience at L. L. Bean, they both landed jobs at a well-known shop making Shaker-inspired furniture. There they learned an enormous amount, refined their skills, and discovered where their interests lay in the six years (slightly longer for Rodel) they were there. But "progress" came to the shop. "When we started," Rodel relates, "there were just seven cabinetmakers and six chair makers. We worked on each piece from start to finish. But then it was turned into more of a factory—there are 100 people working there now—and we realized the end was coming."

The decision to go it alone was arrived at "reluctantly" Rodel says. "Looking back, we were crazy to do it. But we felt we had no choice."

"We don't get paid sick days anymore," says Mack, "but you make choices and you live with them."

In their wooden, partially post-and-beam shop just 100 feet from their home on their wooded forty-acre property, Rodel is the design genius—"The things that go on in his brain are many and varied," his wife says appreciatively—while Mack works with him part-time. Having their own shop has allowed her to pursue other interests: music and community involvement. She was elected two terms in a row as town selectman in Pownal, Maine, the first woman to hold the job. "Our community is our lifeblood. We live here and work here, and being part of our community is part of our life." Mack also plays the bagpipes at weddings and funerals, having given up the fiddle when she realized, contrary to what she'd been told as

The Argyll Server from Mack & Rodel—modeled on a 1904 washstand by Charles Rennie Mackintosh—features a leaded-art-glass back and a countertop of Chinese Blue Fulper tiles.

a child, that women really could play the pipes. They raise their two sons together.

"I do miss the time in the shop," Mack admits. "Every time I go in there, Kevin has something great going on." "Something great" includes a Harvey Ellis-inspired bookcase with handblown glass and inlay work; Frank Lloyd Wright-flavored desks and settles; and a Glasgow sideboard and coffee table. Glasgow school-inspired pieces take their design vocabulary not just from Mackintosh's work but from the work of lesser-known members of the Glasgow school, such as Mackintosh's wife, Margaret MacDonald, her sister, Frances MacDonald, and Frances's husband, Herbert McNair. A unique design typical of Rodel is a major dining table featuring inset art tiles, Mackintosh-inspired grid-patterned cross-stretchers, and corner pillars adapted from Frank Lloyd Wright's Robie House table.

The furniture-grade hardwoods come from specialty sawyers, mostly in the mid-Atlantic and Midwest. Oak pieces are fumed, or exposed to vapors of concentrated ammonia that color the wood naturally without disguising the rich grain. All pieces are finished with three to six coats of linseed oil.

The craftsmen feel they've struck a good balance between machine and handwork. "We use the table saw to cut and dimension rough stock to size, for example. To do so by hand would take an extraordinary amount of time and may be inconsistent or inaccurate. Conversely," they say, "we have yet to find a machine that executes a set of dovetails as artfully as the human hand and eye." Except for hardware and stained glass and tile insets, which are produced by other specialty craftsmen, "we do everything ourselves, right down to the finish."

Things almost changed recently when the Glasgow School of Art discovered their work via the Internet and contacted them about producing a line of Mackintosh reproductions from their collection. Initially interested, Mack and Rodel ended up passing on the opportunity. "Even at low quantities—even forty pieces at a time—it was more than we could make in a year," Rodel explains. "It would have meant changing the nature of the business, getting a bigger shop, hiring employees. So," he shrugs, "we're still doing it the slower but more traditional way."

Michael McGlynn
Prairie School Furniture

Like most midwesterners, Michael McGlynn grew up well aware of the genius of Frank Lloyd Wright. His parents kept illustrated books on the architect around their home in rural Wisconsin, and one could not partake of city life without being somewhat aware of Wright's contributions and influence on twentieth-century design.

As a result, when McGlynn moved to Minneapolis after college and started his own woodworking company, he was quite surprised to discover a whole range of talents obscured by the luminous glow of Frank Lloyd Wright. Today, although McGlynn appreciates the designer's aesthetic as much as anyone, his handmade furniture sings the praises of the lesser-known—but not necessarily lesser—talents of the Prairie School in the early decades of this century.

"The more I do this, the more I realize there's a whole untapped world out here of people who've disappeared off the map. You go to a bookstore and there are hundreds of books on Wright and none on these other people."

The "other people" include Minneapolis-based architects George Grant Elmslie, who for many years was Louis Sullivan's chief draftsman, and his business partner William Gray Purcell. Walter Burley Griffin, a notable architect married to another accomplished architect, was just one of a whole group of architects who were based in the same Chicago office building as Wright. Griffin homes were "very massive, with a kind of rusticated look to them, with lots of heavy stone," McGlynn relates. His career in America ended in the early teens when he won a competition to design a capitol building for Australia and became a prominent architect there.

It is the work of Purcell and Elmslie with which McGlynn has become the most closely identified. A lifelong woodworker who learned from his father, an accomplished hobbyist, McGlynn worked in a boat-building shop and as a cabinetmaker before succeeding in turning furniture making into a full-time

job a decade ago. His first Prairie-style furniture clients came through an architectural firm with whom McGlynn had shared his portfolio. For their Greene & Greene-style home he got his first big commission: a Frank Lloyd Wright-inspired dining-room table and chairs. "Since then I've done many, many pieces for them. They've since moved to Colorado, but I still make furniture for them."

His second "big break" followed on the heels of the first. "The Purcell-Cutts House in Minneapolis, which is owned by the Minneapolis Institute of Art, was Purcell's own house," McGlynn explains. "He designed it, although he only lived there a few years. It's a very striking Prairie School house, with horizontal lines and leaded-glass windows. By the time it was donated, all of the

This Frank Lloyd Wright-inspired sideboard, with proportions taken from a Greene & Greene sideboard, was built by McGlynn to match an existing dining-room set whose table was based on Wright's Allen House and whose chairs were based on Wright's Husser House. Made of cherry rather than the white oak Wright favored, the sideboard's feet match those of the Husser House table, as does the applied raised banding that wraps around the corners.

original furniture was gone. I read that the Institute was having some chairs replicated by a furniture maker in Chicago and contacted the curator."

The curator was impressed enough by the quality of McGlynn's work that when the money was available for further refurbishing, McGlynn was hired to build all the furniture for a bedroom. "Through that job," he says, "I've become associated with Purcell and Elmslie and have ended up doing a lot of Purcell and Elmslie furniture."

He has produced furniture for a number of Purcell and Elmslie houses in the Twin Cities area, and has also made furniture for the architects' most famous house, built in 1911 in Wood's Hole, Massachusetts. "It's the one that's always in the books. It's in an incredible location, on a spit of land jutting into the ocean looking out towards Martha's Vineyard. It's very linear—the locals nicknamed it the 'airplane house'—with cypress siding in bands that give it a ribbonlike effect. It's very dramatic."

Purcell and Elmslie's houses, built mostly between 1905 and 1920, he says, "range from really dramatic to real ordinary but with lots of little design features. They were very prolific architects. They designed houses and furniture for very wealthy clients, but they did a lot for middle-income clients where they just built the house, like one they built for Purcell's piano tuner. Financially they were very successful—unlike Wright."

The furniture that was designed for these striking and dramatic houses is immediately identifiable as Prairie School: cube-framed chairs with spindle sides, for instance. Their work differs from, say, Wright's in the signature use of blocks between the spindles, a favorite motif, and, sometimes, wooden balls at the bases of the chairs.

Photograph courtesy the artist.

Having grown up in the Midwest, Michael McGlynn has been strongly influenced by the work of the Prairie School designers, particularly Frank Lloyd Wright, and George Grant Elmslie and William Gray Purcell.

McGlynn worked from both photographs and Elmslie's original full-scale drawings to make this replica of a Purcell and Elmslie dining chair from the T. B. Keith House in Eau Claire, Wisconsin. Its V-shaped back with cutout shows the influence of Louis Sullivan, who employed a lot of stylized organic tracery cutout, and for whom Elmslie had worked.

Photograph courtesy the artist.

"The repetitive spindles with blocks were everywhere in Purcell and Elmslie's architecture," McGlynn says. "There's practically nothing that doesn't have that in some variation somewhere. At the Purcell-Cutts House, for instance, it's in the fence. They were always using little variations on the same theme. Another thing that sets them apart, particularly in a lot of their furniture, is a kind of tracery cutout that appears in the backs of chairs. You'll see it repeated in a lot of furniture and homes. In almost every one of their homes I've been in, I've seen something like that somewhere. The beams in a house might have a tracery cutout applied to them. The Cape Cod house has incredible interior detailing like that. The cutouts are often adaptations of a plant design, a little like some of Wright's windows that are plantlike but very geometric. This is the same idea, but mostly as curved lines that are adapted to a geometric form. In that way, they were similar to some of the things Mackintosh was doing."

It is unclear, though, who their influences were, McGlynn says. "I went two summers ago to a Mackintosh show in Chicago, and there were real eerie similarities between his work and Purcell and Elmslie. But nowhere is there an indication that they'd seen each other's work."

Like many fine woodworkers, McGlynn is also inspired by the work of southern California architects Greene & Greene. "I had only known about them in tidbits until I made furniture for a client whose house was in the Greene & Greene style. I borrowed all his books and started studying them and became very enthused about their work. The level of detail is just on another plane. A lot of Wright's stuff was really poorly made; Purcell and Elmslie's furniture was pretty well made. But Greene & Greene crossed the line into being art. As someone who works with wood, I can really appreciate the level of craftsmanship that went into everything they made, from a light-switch plate to a piece of furniture. It's really amazing, especially considering the size of their shop, where the workers were working for their paycheck every Friday. And their work is so beautiful, too—it's structural *and* beautiful," he says.

"Woodworkers often have a disdain for furniture created by architects because it usually doesn't work. I had an architect bring me a design for a table, and if I'd built it that way, it would have cracked apart the minute the humidity changed one degree. Frank Lloyd Wright's furniture was strictly aesthetic. A chair was art; it wasn't meant to be used as a chair. But Greene & Greene were different; they understood the medium. They were woodworkers, after all. And their work today, unless it has been abused, is almost as good as the day it was built."

McGlynn is especially interested in many of the smaller Greene & Greene-designed items—clocks and lights, for instance—that aren't getting as much attention as their chairs and tables. Lately he has also found himself drawn increasingly to the designs of Charles Rennie Mackintosh and the Viennese Secessionists, such as Josef Hoffman.

"I try to design pieces that have some elements and the feel of those designers but are original. Lately I've been working on lamps that have the feel of Purcell and Elmslie, although I know of only one lamp they ever made. There's a world of choices out there. I'm not terribly interested in making fifty copies of the same thing," McGlynn says. "I was contacted about making Stickley-type Morris chairs—seventy-five of them—for a lodge, and I said no way. I'd be happy to make one or two, but not seventy-five. I'm happy doing what I'm doing. I keep plenty

Facing
Frank Lloyd Wright-style dining-room set by Michael McGlynn.

Photograph courtesy the artist.

Photograph © Matt Prince.

An Arts & Crafts settle by Stockton unites the classic Stickley form in cherry with Greene & Greene-influenced detailing of ebony and sterling silver.

Facing
McGlynn's reproduction of a Purcell and Elmslie chair in white oak plants their work firmly in the Prairie School—in the chair's cube-like shape, for instance, and its use of spindles. But the designers made it their own with distinctive details such as the balls at its base and the introduction of blocks protruding between the spindles.

busy and I get to pick and choose what I want to do."

"For me," says Michael McGlynn, "the joy and interest comes from making something new."

Thomas Starbuck Stockton
Arts & Crafts Originals

Some craftsmen mark their shops with a sign announcing their craft, or at least a home adorned with their work. But the sign of the craftsman at Tom Stockton's last home, in Santa Rosa, California, were the chairs hung up along an old fence line that marked his backyard. His son's friends thought they were funky, and the neighbors . . . perhaps they were relieved when he moved away. As for Stockton, well, whenever he needed firewood he could simply pull one off the fence and break it up.

There *is* an explanation. Since every design is original, Stockton usually won't make a chair without first working out a design on paper and then building a prototype. Since he makes them out of the shop's scrap wood, he doesn't hesitate to give them a third and last life as firewood. He can design on paper, of course, but when an object is on a piece of paper he can't walk around it and see it from all sides. He can't sit on it, either. Thus, the design process starts in the head, gets interpreted on paper, and is further defined in the prototype. But the final refinement of the design—where the magic happens—goes on in Stockton's head. Somewhere within the interaction of head, heart, and hands, a unique piece is born each time. "Good workmanship goes hand in hand with good design," he explains. "Both are necessary to create beautiful furniture that will last over lifetimes."

41

A descendant of Arts & Crafts architect Louis Easton, Thomas Starbuck Stockton's Asian-influenced sensibility was established during his childhood in Korea, where he was surrounded by Asian antiques.

Photograph © 1999 Chase Reynolds Ewald.

A Stickley-inspired settle that the clients wanted "lightened up" and given some Greene & Greene influence; an overtly Asian desk with handmade drawer pulls and rice-paper doors on its small cabinets; a set of chairs based on one in the Greenes' Thorsen House but with a distinctive inlay design accommodating the client's preferences—every piece is signature Stockton. This makes him a favorite with both Arts & Crafts galleries such as the Craftsman's Guild in San Francisco and contemporary woodworking galleries such as Highlight Gallery in Mendocino. As for straight reproductions, he says, "I'm much too obsessive. If I were going to do an exact copy, I would get totally wrapped up in trying to do it *right*."

A Californian, Stockton lived in Palo Alto until he was seven, then in southern California. When he was in fourth grade, his father's business relocated the family to South Korea for two years. The experience had a lasting effect on Stockton, most notably on his sense of aesthetics. "We lived in Seoul. It was an interesting place to grow up. I learned to bargain and swear in Korean." He also learned to appreciate the delicate beauty of

Asian furniture. "My parents bought a lot of furniture when we were there. Instead of growing up with Early American furniture, I grew up with Japanese and Korean antiques." This is evident today in his use of cloud-lift details (heavily used by Greene & Greene, too) and Asian-influenced drawer pulls.

Santa Barbara was next on the itinerary, followed by New Jersey, where Stockton attended high school. There he had his first woodworking experience. He says simply, "It was one of the first things I ever did that I felt competent at."

He had found his calling. When his parents moved to Michigan (they've now settled down on an organic orange orchard in southern California), Stockton took the offer of a job and place to live with some family friends who made hand-carved redwood outdoor furniture in Sonoma County. After four years with what he calls his "extended family," he decided it was time to refine his skills further. He enrolled in a fine-woodworking course at College of the Redwoods in Fort Bragg, California, followed by a year at the Primrose Center, a small furniture-making school in Missoula, Montana.

"For the first ten weeks we used only hand tools, plus the band saw and drill press. We worked on our tools and learned joinery techniques, like mortise-and-tenon and dovetails. We made a little box with a drawer—and then they turned us loose on the machines." The school's focus on woodworking was important for his craft, Stockton recalls, "but it didn't teach you how to deal with the realities of what you need to be successful, like dealing with clients." Consequently, he landed two apprenticeships with master woodworkers through the Baulines Craft Guild, first with C. Stuart Welch, where he focused on design through drawing and learned to operate a business. Under David J. Marks he studied advanced finishing techniques.

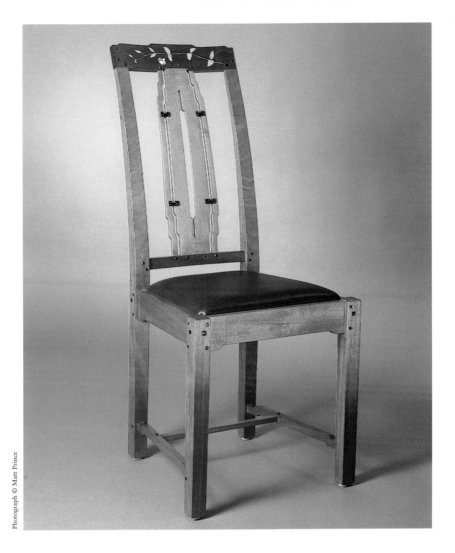

Photograph © Matt Prince

Tom Stockton's Greene & Greene-inspired chair is both graceful and intricately detailed, with mahogany, ebony, silver, mother-of-pearl, abalone, pearwood, and oak.

After that, he was on his own. Stockton rented a barn in rural Sonoma County "for $85 a month, including utilities," he recalls fondly. There he set out to make the furniture that would associate his name with fine craftsmanship and unique design. At first, he says, "I starved." But he had subcontract work from the redwood-furniture company, and he learned during this time not to turn away jobs. (Once, in fact, he repaired a rocker for a kid who had needed a handle for his paint-ball gun, and had turned to his dad's furniture as a convenient source of wood.) He made pieces of his own design and let the work speak for itself to several

different galleries in northern California. He began showing at venues such as the California Contemporary Crafts Association, the Sonoma County Woodworkers' Association, and the Marin Society of Artists. And he started winning awards—every year except one, in fact, since he went out on his own in 1988.

Stockton lives with his wife and son in mountainous Shasta County, in a house made from a water tank that a glassblower relocated from the East Bay Hills. There, they live at 3,000 feet, watching wildlife in the summer and watching the snow pile up in the winter. He divides his time between commission work for clients, many of whom are repeat customers, and works that come out of his own interests and desires at a particular moment. He enjoys the balance.

It is ironic that, although Stockton had been making furniture for thirteen years and had been focusing on Arts & Crafts-style furniture for the previous three years, he didn't completely realize his own Arts & Crafts heritage until he found himself at the groundbreaking exhibition chronicling California's Arts & Crafts history at the Oakland Museum in 1994. "I went down there to see the show, and I was looking at a small stool and reading the description, and said, 'Hey, that's my great-grandfather!'" Louis Easton, a Pasadena architect and sometime furniture designer, built Arts & Crafts houses with a Mission influence. Easton's brother-in-law was the great soap-salesman-turned-Arts-&-Crafts-proselytizer Elbert Hubbard.

In the furniture of Thomas Starbuck Stockton, the Arts & Crafts movement really has come full circle.

Debey Zito
Furniture Inspired by Greene & Greene and the Far East

Six women cluster around a table in the workshop-basement of Debey Zito's San Francisco home. Heads bent over their notebooks, they take notes in respectful silence. Zito's dog lies by the door, barking at the late arrival, while a white rabbit with gray ears hops quietly along the floor, exploring students' bags. Scattered across the table are books with titles like *Understanding Wood, Building with Nature,* and *The Soul of a Tree.*

Debey Zito is talking about joinery, the often invisible aspect of furniture making that is every bit as important, at least to her, as the look of the finished piece when viewed across a room. To her, a piece can't be beautiful if it isn't functional, and it can't be functional if it isn't built to last. "In Arts & Crafts, the engineering is part of the design," she says. "The way something goes together is integral to how it looks."

She starts at the beginning, describing joinery as "the basis of furniture making." She lists the elements of joinery (glue and mechanized holds, dovetails and mortise-and-tenon, rabbet joints and dados), and explains wood in terms of its cellular structure so that the students can understand how it continues to move, shrink, and expand with temperature and humidity. Then she goes on to say, "I'm going to tell you the rules, then tell you how to break them."

Zito is not just a highly regarded Arts & Crafts furniture maker, she is a teacher too. Perhaps in an attempt to level the field for women in woodworking, perhaps as a reaction to her own experience trying to be taken seriously as a woman woodworker, she teaches only women. Her select apprentices, too, are always female. There's a reason.

Photograph © Andy Freeberg.

Craftswoman Debey Zito is both teacher and environmental advocate who says every piece of furniture should be built to last at least two hundred years.

Above

A close-up of Debey Zito's "bat bed" shows the artistry of the carving detail by craftswoman Terry Schmitt.

Right

Debey Zito's "bat bed" made of sustainably grown kwilla, a tropical hardwood, was designed for an antiques collector from the Cotswolds who wanted to evoke the feeling of the English Arts & Crafts movement.

Had she loved woodworking with any less passion, Zito would certainly have faltered, become a confirmed "weekend workshopper" by the time she was finished with that first high school woodworking class almost thirty years ago. That was the one in which, when she enrolled, the teacher said, "I knew with women's lib we'd get a girl in here eventually." Upon graduating from high school, she called every cabinetmaking shop in Los Angeles looking for a job; usually she was laughed at. "It was a really humiliating experience," she recalls. She studied botany at Sonoma State University, following her secondary passion, nature. When a professor

wisely advised her to pursue what she loved most, she transferred to San Diego State University, where she was one of only five women out of 500 industrial-arts students. In metalworking, she says, "The professor bothered me every day for wearing a dress to welding class."

In fairness, though, both teachers gave her a chance. The high school teacher "was fantastic. He let me in; he didn't have to. My first piece he made me sand down to my knuckles. By senior year I was spending half my time in woodshop, and I won an award. It came with a little money, but it was more the

Debey Zito's original maple tansu, a fusion of Asian and Arts & Crafts influences, bears a contemporary yet timeless look.

students to pass the final when her welds successfully withstood 60,000 pounds of pressure.)

From her vantage point now as an acknowledged master craftsman and much-sought-after woodworking teacher, Zito can afford to be generous. "The experience made me a better craftsman because I had to do it perfectly to get past any strength problems." Of the sexist attitudes: "I survived that in spite of what I had to go through because," she says simply, "I really loved woodworking."

Although inspired by the work of California Arts & Crafts masters Greene & Greene—in their grace, their mastery of form and composition, their hint of the Orient, and their overall feeling of lightness—Debey Zito's pieces bear a signature style that make them her own. The most strikingly original examples are her chairs, which often feature bird silhouettes inset into the sides of the seats. Recently, she was selected to build pews for the choir loft of the Swedenborgian Church, one of San Francisco's most famous Arts & Crafts structures. For this, she sought an English feel, incorporating a near-Gothic arch in the backs of the pews that echoes the structural woodwork in the church itself. Often she collaborates on projects with partner Terry Schmitt, whose lifelike carvings of animals and plants create striking motifs for mirrors, bookends, and, most recently, an Asian cabinet piece with carved tops.

Zito never gave up her passion for nature, and it is evident in both her resume (she is president of the Golden Gate Audubon Society) and her work. An avowed environmentalist, Zito does most of her designing in her head, while hiking. She's conscientious about the wood she uses, saying, "You buy a piece from me, and yes, a tree was cut down, but every day that it's used—for a couple hundred years—that's a tree that doesn't get cut down. You see Chinese furniture that's been

acknowledgement that mattered." And the college welding instructor, she recalls, "was great. He apologized." (He had to. The first girl in a decade to take an advanced metal-working class, Zito was one of only two

around since the fifth century. There's no reason not to have furniture like that today."

She builds her furniture to last and demands the same of her students—which is why all her beginning woodworking classes include a two-hour lecture on engineering. An integral part of this is her "rain forest rap," a talk on rain forest ecology that explains why no one should buy a piece of tropical hardwood unless it has been harvested through

sustainable forestry practices. Her favorite wood of all is an American native, cherry. "You can see such depth and luster in the wood," she enthuses.

Whatever wood one chooses, one must be respectful, she insists. "Any tree that you're going to use took at least a hundred years to grow. Out of respect for the environment, you absolutely *have* to put together something that will last a hundred years."

A writing desk and chair by Zito reveal a solid Greene & Greene foundation but with an overall lightness. The chair reflects a Chinese influence in the way its legs tenon into mortises in the horizontal top rail.

METALWORK

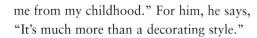

Michael Adams
Dirk van Erp-style Metalwork

Michael Adams is probably the best-known craftsman working in hand-hammered copper today. His signature Dirk van Erp-style table lamps—copper bases bearing the artisan's hammer marks, with shades made of metal and mica—are perhaps more refined than the originals and sing the praises of the Arts & Crafts movement at its height.

Something about the lamps—the rich glow of their copper, their earthy shapes and materials, the fact that they shed a warm light, encouraging thoughtful conversation and contemplative reading—takes one back to the days almost a century ago when thousands of home owners across the country were seeking the simple life made rich through a quality home environment.

Because Adams grew up in "suburbia" of upstate New York, in the generic blandness of a basic fifties American home, he was strongly affected each time he visited his grandparents' Arts & Crafts home.

"It was a later one," says the artist, "but it had the chandelier, the fireplace, built-in bookcases, a repoussé clock over the fireplace, a dining room with the plate railing, oak woodwork. For me, growing up in a suburban house without even molding, and then visiting my grandparents . . . their place even smelled different. My grandfather smoked a pipe, and every time I went there I had the feeling of stepping back in time. I loved that. Now when I see things that are Arts & Crafts, or I visit Gustav Stickley's Craftsman Farms, I get a feeling that reawakens things in

me from my childhood." For him, he says, "It's much more than a decorating style."

Growing up, Adams knew about Arts & Crafts. He also knew how to build things, both instinctively and through more formal training. He learned mechanics from his dad, and in his free time was always, it seemed, building forts, tree houses, clubhouses. He loved shop class in junior high. "I was an odd character," Adam laughs. "I made my own electric guitar. I even made my own frets. Not that I was musically inclined! Of course," he admits, "it didn't work very well, but it worked."

It took him a while to find his calling, though. At first he thought he might be a mechanic, then he decided he wanted to be an artist. "I bought canvas and paints and applied to art school. Of course I was rejected," he laughs. He did go so far as to try to sell his landscapes door-to-door when he was still in high school. "It was so humili-ating, but it did teach me a valuable lesson. You need to put your energy into something people want. I decided I could apply my design sense, my creativity, to another medium."

Adams enrolled at Syracuse University to study design but "really hated it. It wasn't what I imagined." He was still interested in classical art, though, so he spent all his time in the library doing independent research. "Any design sense that I have," he says, "comes from that research."

Adams worked with wood and cast bronze before getting involved with glass. There he thought he had found his medium, entranced

Facing
The classic designs of Dirk van Erp serve as lasting inspiration for Michael Adams, whose table lamps are of hand-hammered copper with mica shades.

Aurora Studios offers several styles of chandelier, this one based on a design by August Tiesselinck, Dirk van Erp's nephew.

as he was by the marriage of color and design and its unlimited variations. "In stained glass there are a million possibilities for what a lamp or window could be, everything from medieval to Art Deco. There's a tremendous range."

For years he did restoration work on Victorian windows and lamps, and also tried his hand at making lamps; a typical work was an oak lamp base with a pyramidal stained-glass shade. But he hadn't lost his interest in Arts & Crafts and had, in fact, become a collector, even though he was struggling financially. "Back in the seventies, it wasn't collectible," he explains. "That was way back before anyone wanted it. You could

buy generic Mission furniture for nothing. It was great."

Through his work and his interest in Arts & Crafts, he came to the attention of New York Tiffany collector and author Egon Neustadt, who had been collecting Tiffany stained glass since the 1940s. Adams worked on restoring Neustadt's "hundreds" of lamps for the next six years.

"I really learned a lot," Adams reflects. "Tiffany is at the highest level of glasswork. It would teach me, and I would teach myself. I started doing some of my own work, but using central New York as my customer base was an awful way to try to have a business. My first customer was a professor at Oswego

University who had written a book about Maxfield Parrish and Arts & Crafts in New York State. So it was a pretty specialized, limited market. With this type of work, you need a larger area to sell to."

But he kept at it through the seventies and eighties. "I lived very simply, and it was always a struggle to make ends meet. I always put too much into each piece. Every step was a big step. And this was simple stuff. But I tried. I tried hard."

One day in 1985, an antiques dealer from California came by the shop. "Jerry Cohen dropped off a Gustav Stickley chandelier and challenged me to make one," he remembers. Adams rose to the challenge. "I kind of used everything I'd learned," he recalls. He also found that he loved working with metal even more than working with glass. He and Cohen became a team: Adams would make the chandeliers and, later, lamps and sconces, and Cohen would find a home for them. The partnership continues to this day and helped push the growth of Adams's shop from a one-man endeavor to the point where he employs several craftspeople.

Adams's work in various areas of craftsmanship serves him in good stead now, he says. "I did all these different things, which I don't regret. I'm able to talk shop with a lot of different people. I can relate to what they do. I can deal with foundries, for instance, and understand what it takes to do something. But I know better than to do too many different things."

His facility for understanding how things work has made it natural for him to embrace technology. A self-professed computer buff, Adams does much of his design work on the computer. "I'm a *modern* craftsperson," he insists. "I may be doing old designs, but I'd be a fool not to take advantage of technology. I was talking to a glass bender the other

This hanging lantern—a hand-blown glass cylinder surmounted by a conical hand-formed cap—shows the influence of designer Harvey Ellis in its sculptural ribbon motif.

Michael Adams's signature Dirk van Erp-style table lamps—copper bases bearing the artisan's hammer marks, with shades made of metal and mica—are perhaps more refined than the originals, singing the praises of the movement at its height.

day whose tolerances are an eighth of an inch; I was shocked. I'm within a hair between the meeting of metal and glass. I could never do that without machines. People may criticize, but the old, hard way is not necessarily better."

Although copper is his medium, he has been feeling the urge to flex his wings design-wise.

His long history with Arts & Crafts, he says, "has been like an apprenticeship. But I want to make really outstanding pieces that go way beyond what's been done before."

In the meantime, Michael Adams, along with his wife, Dawn Hopkins, creates a team effort with the other craftspeople at Aurora Studios. Many of the artisans who work at the shop come from artistic backgrounds and bring skills of their own—a satisfying reward, Adams says.

"In the sixties and the seventies, copper was a lost art. It had its heyday, then it faded away. In the twenties there were all these talented people, but the depression hit and in one generation all that knowledge was lost. It must have been very sad for those people who had all this skill and no work," Adams reflects. "People like me had to learn the hard way. But I feel really lucky that we're in a time and place that people appreciate this work."

Buffalo Studios
Glass Lighting

The name may be Buffalo, but the place resembles a rabbit's warren.

Just beyond the deceptively ordered office entry area of this metalworking shop not far from southern California's John Wayne

Airport, the visitor steps into a vast work space that seems a hive of activity whether one person is at work or ten, as is often the case. A twisting, turning trip takes one through aisles of lathes, milling machines, and grinders; templates, drill bits, and tools too numerous to list; cabinets containing drawers upon drawers of tiny handmade metal parts. (Square-headed rivets, for instance. "They have to have this kind of head to get this look," says owner Greg Bowman. "You can't buy 'em, so you make 'em." They even make their own doorknobs, hooks, and chain links, which are cast from molds they carve by hand.)

Utilitarian metal shelves are stacked high with long rods of soldering metals; sheets of brass, copper, mica, and glass; wooden mushroom-shaped molds (used for laying out intricate Tiffany-glass patterns); forms for wrapping chain links; and thousands of mylar patterns for cutting the glass for leaded-glass lamp shades. A row of shelves nestled up against the ceiling holds labeled boxes, each containing critical components from each different job in case they ever get asked to make another. Of course, there are anvils.

Everywhere one looks is evidence of work in progress: intricately cutout copper sheets for four-sided outdoor lanterns, cast-bronze bases for lamps that would strain your back to lift, hanging lanterns awaiting the final patina, a

Photograph © Stan Sholik.

The thirty-year-old Buffalo Studios—a cooperative venture whose figureheads are owner Greg Bowman (front right) and master craftsman Tony Smith (front left)—is known for its meticulous reproductions of the work of Louis Comfort Tiffany, Greene & Greene, and western designer Thomas Molesworth. Even the chain links are cast from hand-carved molds.

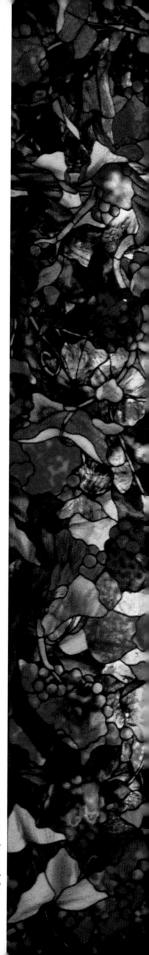

Photograph courtesy Buffalo Studios.

Buffalo Studios adapted a Tiffany design to make this twelve-light floor-standing Lily Lamp. The base is cast bronze, the lily shades hand-blown.

large bronze eagle, and, back by the door to the office, rows of fabulously colored hand-blown glass shades. A small showroom boasts hanging lanterns of all Arts & Crafts descriptions, stained-glass light panels, assorted hardware, fireplace tools, Tiffany reproduction candlesticks, and a section of railing for a celebrity's one-of-a-kind Art Nouveau home.

"Well," shrugs Bowman, founder of this thirty-year-old, cooperative venture in metal-working artistry, "you can never anticipate what the customer wants, so we try to keep a cross section. You can go to a lighting store and get what everyone else has or you can

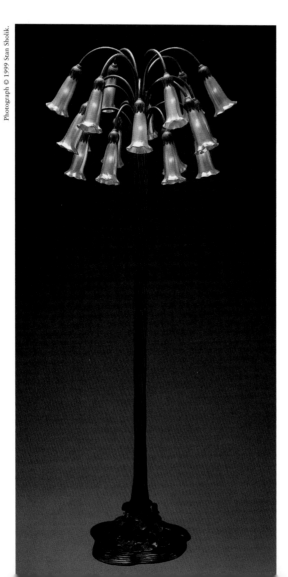

Photograph © 1999 Stan Sholik.

come here and get something different. We encourage people to come look. It's not something you can impart over the phone."

Indeed. On the other hand, even a trip through the workshop doesn't do justice to Buffalo Studios' nearly three decades of metalwork. Bowman founded the company in Pasadena in 1972 with Bob Tatosian; when EPA regulations made life too difficult for them to continue operating their foundry and plating shop, they split up. Tatosian went off to found Arroyo Craftsman, a manufacturing company that ships Arts & Crafts lighting fixtures all over the country. Since then Bowman and company have produced everything from the lanterns for the Greene brothers' Blacker House, along with restoration work on many other Greene & Greene houses, ("Our work is historically correct," says metalworker Richard Boukes, "but better"), to re-creations of western designer Thomas Molesworth's chandeliers with Indians on horseback chasing buffalo around a tepee. They have made hundreds of detailed cutout copper lanterns and sconces. Reproduction Tiffany lamps with cast bases and delicately leaded stained-glass shades have been a staple from the beginning. Recently, they constructed an indoor spiral staircase made entirely of iron in the shape of a grapevine, complete with grape clusters and birds.

"We started out specializing in Tiffany reproductions, then we got into Greene & Greene, then a little Frank Lloyd Wright," says Bowman. "We haven't done just one thing. We've branched out as tastes have changed."

Buffalo Studios' artisans have completed an enormous amount of restoration work on original Tiffany, Stickley, Frank Lloyd Wright, and Dirk van Erp pieces—but virtually none on their own work. Their new work is built to last, using the best materials available. Which is good, because with

A post-mounted Arts & Crafts lantern of leaded glass and copper-plated brass shows a Mackintosh influence.

Buffalo Studios, there is no such thing as instant gratification. "We're pretty low production," says artisan Tony Smith, "because everything takes forever to make. We used to advertise, but we stopped to catch up. We haven't advertised in five years—and we still haven't caught up. In fact," he adds, "we're busier than ever."

Still, Buffalo Studios is the only choice for many knowing architects, designers, and home owners. Their client list boasts such personalities as George Lucas, Steven Spielberg, Sony CEO Peter Guber, best-selling author Dean Koontz, producer Joel Silver (who owns two original Frank Lloyd Wright homes), and a long list of antiques collectors. And they're all repeat customers. But Bowman is quick to point out, "The people who've kept the Buffalo rolling aren't famous. They're people from all walks of life, from every level, who have supported us from the beginning."

"The Buff," as the regulars call it, is more like a cooperative than a company, and much like a family. Greg Bowman was there first, of course, but Cliff Mathieson has handled all the artwork since the early seventies; for two decades Debbie Rupe has provided the steady hand and good eye required for cutting the glass that becomes the intricate Tiffany-reproduction shades and windows; Richard Boukes met Buffalo Studios through his iron-work in 1983; Bowman's dad, Richard Bowman, has worked there off and on for years since his retirement from the aerospace industry. Master metalworker Tony Smith has been involved since the late eighties. Explains Boukes, "We're all really independent, but we collaborate on joint projects."

And then there are the long-term relationships with other custom shops. One small foundry does their sand casting; another handles the works requiring the lost-wax process. When the occasion demands it, there is another custom shop that does metal spinning. Bowman's relationships with glass suppliers and custom glassblowers goes back decades. "We have to depend on these other craftsmen who really know their job," Bowman says. "They can do things when everyone else says, 'Nah, I don't know how to do that.' "

And when they get a really major job that needs to be completed right away, Tony Smith says, "Greg's got a network of old buddies, metalworkers who like to come back and work intensively for four or five days, then go back to horse ranching or whatever."

The team evolved over the course of years. Boukes, an ornamental ironworker who met Bowman in 1983 on a major metalworking job, recalls his first impression. "I was just enamored of Buffalo Studios. It was a total shop. They had everything: glass, plating, a foundry, machine shop, drafting rooms—

everything from start to finish. It was really impressive."

Tony Smith first went to the Gamble House in 1970, a moment of enlightenment that caused him to "throw away" a computer-programming job in order to build custom houses. The other effect, he says, was that "I became a Stickley collector about ten minutes after visiting the Gamble House." He met Bowman in the late eighties, he recalls. "I was sick of building houses and Greg needed some copper work. I stupidly said I'd do it, not realizing what I was getting into."

"I told him the truth," Bowman says. "I said, 'It'll ruin your marriage, you'll work all the time, and you'll make no money.' "

Smith nods. "I've thrown away lots of careers, but I'm much happier."

Clearly a passion for the work unites the group. Attests Tony Smith, "If we had all the money in the world, we'd be doing exactly what we do now."

Chris Efker
Hand-Hammered Hardware

Chris Efker is living proof that one doesn't need to be located in an Arts & Crafts "hot spot" to be a vital member of the Arts & Crafts Revival. He started his hand-hammered-hardware company just as he was moving from Pasadena, California, a mecca for Arts & Crafts enthusiasts, to Marceline, Missouri, a farming community of 2,400 whose closest city is Kansas City, two hours away.

It might have seemed crazy at the time. He left behind a brand new Greene & Greene-style home he had built with his own hands from bottom to top, outside in (from electrical and plumbing systems to windowsills and lighting fixtures), and a successful career

Efker has expanded his line to include vases based on Karl Kipp's designs and hand-hammered Arts & Crafts clocks.

Doorknobs and handles, drawer pulls and light-switch plates, each bearing hundreds of hammer marks catching and reflecting the light, make up Efker's line of handmade hardware.

as a remodeling contractor. He had a wife and three daughters to support. But he knew he wanted to do something more meaningful for his life's work, and he and his wife agreed they didn't want to raise their children amid the problems of semi-urban America.

They chose Missouri simply because that's where Efker's parents-in-law were living; Efker chose to focus on hardware after a stint at making Arts & Crafts lighting because he felt there was a need for it, and he hadn't seen anyone else offering the kind of custom quality he felt he could offer.

While his wife went ahead and moved to Missouri, Efker stayed behind for almost a year taking care of loose ends and making a few contacts that would get him started in business. He stopped by Warren Hile Studio, a successful contemporary Arts & Crafts furniture maker in nearby Sierra Madre. When he showed Hile a chain he had made, the craftsman immediately asked him to make a copper ring on a square plate to be used as a drawer pull for a piece of his furniture. Efker rose to the challenge, "just experimenting until it looked right." Hile became his first customer, initiating a relationship that continues to this day.

Around this time, Efker also secured his first "whole house" job from a woman building a house in Vermont whom he met in the bookstore of Charles and Henry Greene's landmark Gamble House. She was buying lamps and accessories, but when she saw photocopied pictures of Efker's work, she started ordering drawer pulls and light-switch plates until she had furnished the whole house with hardware.

Still, the move was a leap of faith, Efker admits. "At one point, my wife asked me what I was going to do. Meanwhile, her mother was out scoping out work for me in

Photograph courtesy the artist.

construction. I said, 'I'm going to make hardware.' "

He joined his family in Missouri in 1993. For a time, the hardware "was still a garage business, and I was just making enough to get by." Within two years, however, Efker owned two commercial buildings on the main street of Marceline and employed half a dozen people. Today, the Craftsman Hardware Company boasts twelve employees, nine of whom make hardware full-time. They serve hundreds and hundreds of clients each year, from individuals who order one item from the Craftsman Hardware catalog to architects and designers who work closely with Efker to design hardware for entire buildings. A handful of discerning Arts & Crafts furniture craftsmen—such as Warren Hile in southern California and Mack and Rodel in Maine—also depend on Efker for much of the hardware that goes on their case pieces. Although he has developed a line of hardware—expanded in recent years to include Arts & Crafts clocks, frames, and vases—every item is made to order.

Efker, who studied engineering at UCLA before a stint in the service, is totally self-taught in his craft. "I've always liked to work with my hands; I've never had any problem with it. But I had no knowledge of metalworking, and you couldn't go out and find a book or a list of tools that you'd need; they just weren't there. I even had to make my own tools."

Nonetheless, when he started he was so caught up in building his house that he didn't hesitate. "I just made modifications until it looked right. I worked at it until I had a couple of fifty-gallon drums of dead soldiers—meaning I did a lot of experimenting—and just went from there." Efker doesn't draw anything when he's designing ("I already know what it's going to look like before I

Photograph © 1999 Chase Reynolds Ewald.

Chris Efker's no-nonsense approach to the construction of his Greene & Greene-style house led him to create appropriate Arts & Crafts hardware. After much experimentation, he perfected his work and now supplies hardware to individuals and manufacturers across the country.

make it," he explains), although he often works from sketches provided by designers. Efker's team of craftsmen are all trained by him; like him, they showed the aptitude for the work without any specific background in it.

A piece of Craftsman Hardware has a heavy, solid feel and bears the marks of the craftsman's hammer. Hinges and straps can look almost medieval in their thickness and styling as they secure the corners and top of a heavy wooden chest. Trapezoidal vases, patterned after those made by Karl Kipp early in the century, have sloping sides bearing distinctive hammer marks and cutout squares in sets of four running in a band around the top.

A copper door-handle set is a study in functional beauty: its thick, curved, tapering handle invites one's hand to wrap around it and pull; a long, vertical bookplate bears hundreds of hammer marks, each of which catches and reflects the light; four sets of four Mackintosh-style square cutouts punctuate each corner; deckled edges create a distinctive outline.

The door handle may be the first tactile experience a person has upon returning home. A Craftsman Hardware handle—and its message of functional beauty—announces that home is a haven.

Dennis Casey

Frank Lloyd Wright-Inspired Art Glass

While Dennis Casey physically dwells in a modest hillside Bay Area home encroached upon by the suburban sprawl of Silicon Valley, he mentally inhabits a place populated by the irascible genius of the man who was arguably America's greatest twentieth-century designer—Frank Lloyd Wright.

It is hard to pinpoint at what moment Casey's life took this irrevocable turn, at what point he went from being a lifelong woodworking hobbyist to finding full expression—and a career—in Wright's stained-glass designs. It grew on him slowly—in college, in the military, as a draftsman, in the Peace Corps in Peru, and as an engineer—over a period of decades.

"I always worked with wood," Casey said, "from the time I was a kid. Whenever I needed anything for my room, shelves or something, I just built it. I was always a fan of Frank Lloyd Wright; he was always in the background. Then, about twenty-five years ago, I was building a bookcase. I was going to put a piece of plastic in front and it just looked terrible. I thought about glass, and went to the hardware store and got some scraps. . . . A secretary in the office was taking a course in stained glass. I thought I'd take the class, too, so she gave me a list of tools I needed. I got the tools and started working and, well, I never did take the class."

The more he dabbled, the more skilled he became. Soon Casey was copying Wright's windows and "playing around" with Wright's designs. After a few more years, he started on lamps. First he copied Wright's designs from photographs; later he traveled to the Midwest to visit Wright's houses that were open to the public in order to study the pieces firsthand. Ten years later, in the course of repositioning himself for a job change, Casey took a computer course and learned to use a popular professional drafting program. For his term project he chose to draw plans for a double-pedestal lamp from Wright's Dana-Thomas House in Springfield, Illinois.

"This was more ambitious than I needed, but it's what I wanted to do. Then I realized probably other people would be interested, too." He placed some small advertisements for the resulting lamp-building kit in a woodworking magazine and sold enough to immediately start on another lamp from the Dana-Thomas House, this one a single pedestal.

In the meantime, he recalls, "I did take a new job designing airports, but I really wasn't interested in it. What I *was* interested in was Frank Lloyd Wright and stained glass." Thus, a lifelong interest grew into his final career just as his vocation became his avocation.

Casey's plans are sold in glass and woodworking shops around the country, and he has authored four books: *Prairie Art Glass Drawings, Volume I; Prairie Art Glass Drawings, Volume II; Building the Lamps of Frank Lloyd Wright;* and *Art Glass Construction Details of the Dana-Thomas House.* To draft the plans, of course, Casey had to first construct the lamps and windows.

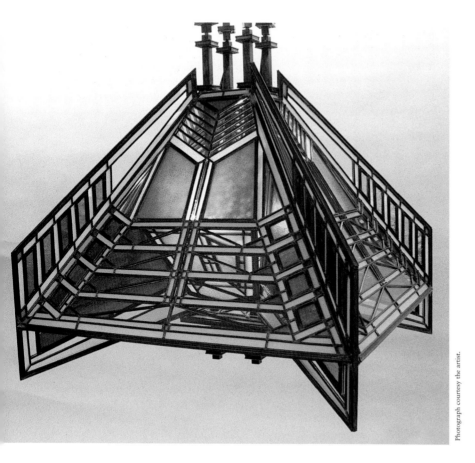

Photograph courtesy the artist.

Casey makes exact replicas as well as modified interpretations, such as in this hanging fixture from Frank Lloyd Wright's Dana House.

Engineer turned art-glass craftsman, Dennis Casey successfully turned his fascination with the glass designs of Frank Lloyd Wright into a career.

Photograph courtesy the artist.

What's most striking when studying his drawings is the unbelievable complexity of the patterns and caming specifications, which Casey has clearly mastered. His craftsmanship is now sought after by the prestigious

Craftsman's Guild Gallery and private collectors around the country.

Casey is one of the foremost experts on Wright's glasswork, though he would shy from such a designation. "There are a lot of historians who could give you the history of art glass more thoroughly than I could," he insists. "But," he concedes, "very few people could tell you what came went into the windows of a house. I could tell you—and give you the stock number."

Years of studying and replicating Wright's designs haven't begun to sate his appetite, he says. "I keep thinking I'm going to run out, but there's no end in sight." Indeed, the Dana-Thomas House alone showcases 450 custom glass panels. "He used certain elements of design over and over, but never the same designs.

"Glass sort of hypnotizes you," Casey says. "I just really enjoy it. When I started out, I thought I could learn it all in a few years. But the more I do, the more I find little subtleties that I didn't see at first."

As owners of his work can attest, this is true even of one piece, one lamp, for instance, with three or four colors of glass on four planes. It can engage the attention moment after moment, year after year, changing as it does with the time of day, the point from which it is viewed, the seasons of nature.

The blues might be variegated, fading in and out and from piece to piece, a slight unevenness and iridescence inviting the play of both natural and artificial light. The blue is interspersed with a hunter green that appears dark as the sea in the daytime but is a glowing virescence when the light shines through at night. The caming divides the planes into sections, then into triangles or chevrons, their repetition and interplay making music of their

own. The caming's organic patterns are stylized, often resembling trees, leaves, flowers, even Froebel's kindergarten cubes. Through Wright's masterful synthesis of color, light, air, and form (even the shadow play of the caming is anticipated), a complete harmony—the ultimate goal of the Arts & Crafts movement—is achieved.

Casey is not a slavish adherent to Wright; he will adapt designs for particular spaces or uses, as in the table lamp enlarged and turned upside down to become a ceiling-mounted dining-room fixture. He will play with the infinite variations on Wright's basic designs, with color sequences, and with the music

inherent in the repetition of patterns. "He innovates on designs," says Barbara Klein, owner of the Craftsman's Guild, "but he retains the essence of Wright. His works, ultimately, are tributes to Frank Lloyd Wright."

In lamps as well as windows, nature is always the unspoken reference point in Casey's glasswork. To both designer and craftsman, glass presents an ingenious, compelling paradox, enclosing space while creating a window to the outside, reflecting in even as we look out. Like the glass itself, Casey's work succeeds in reflecting the genius of Frank Lloyd Wright, while simultaneously making it visible to the world outside.

For the dining room of a Frank Lloyd Wright-inspired home, Casey took a double pedestal lamp from Frank Lloyd Wright's Robie House, 1902, in Springfield, Illinois, enlarged it, turned it upside down, and simplified its design.

Janice McDuffie, the sole potter of Roycroft Potters, operates in a historic Roycroft Building, selling hand-thrown, high-fired porcelain to the pilgrims who come by the thousands to this Arts & Crafts holy ground. As chair of the masters jury of the Roycrofters-at-Large Association, she oversees the process whereby artisans are granted permission to use the Roycroft Renaissance mark.

Janice McDuffie
Roycroft Pottery

April 1995: Janice McDuffie, always nervous before a crowd, stood before a large group assembled at the Roycroft "campus" in East Aurora, New York. She took a deep breath and plunged in.

"I am here tonight, having partially overcome my fear of public speaking, to dispel an even greater fear, that of being spoken for, or about, by some expert who, having never touched clay or fired a kiln, will no doubt try to interpret my chicken pots as something other than just having fun."

The audience must have been surprised, to say the least. After all, McDuffie is the sole Roycroft potter of Roycroft Potters, operating in a historic Roycroft building, selling to the pilgrims who come by the thousands to this Arts & Crafts holy ground. As chair of the masters jury of the Roycrofters-at-Large Association, she oversees the process whereby artisans are given permission to use the Roycroft Renaissance mark. This is serious business.

But that's precisely why McDuffie feels it is important to maintain some perspective.

"There are some people who treat it like God's work," she explains. "And that can become a stranglehold on what you can accomplish. If the play leaves the work, you lose the spark. It's the little things, the small changes, that keep the life in the work."

McDuffie's work has life. Her bowls, pitchers, and many styles of vases possess that quiet solidity that represents both an immediacy and a timelessness. The naturalistic forms—leaves, fish, flowers, dragonflies—that are carved or applied to the thrown pots before glazing and firing add a spirit and uniqueness to each piece.

Her work also evokes a sense of history and a deeply felt Arts & Crafts aesthetic, thanks in large part to the signature deep green matte glaze she spent two years developing. To those in the know, this is ironic. Although ceramics were a major aspect of the Arts & Crafts movement, with major potteries such as Rookwood in Ohio and Grueby Faience in Boston becoming household names and spawning leagues of backyard potters, the most famous Arts & Crafts community of all—Roycroft—produced pottery only briefly in an ill-fated, short-lived experiment.

"The potters—actually, they were painters—only lasted one year. Everyone of that era was just flying by the seat of their pants. They had kiln after kiln of disasters. No one even knows what their work looked like," McDuffie says.

That is just as well, she insists. Kilns are dangerous and old potteries were always burning down; the Roycroft community's fourteen historic buildings, now a National Historic Landmark, might have been vulnerable. Besides, if there had been a distinctive Roycroft pottery line, she might have been confined to reproducing those pots only. She might never have had the chance to develop her own signature style, a process spanning more than two decades.

Arts & Crafts pottery, then and now, draws its inspiration from nature.

Photograph © Jim Via.

Classic forms and a textured matte green glaze that McDuffie spent two years developing provide the stage for a frog among the reeds.

Nineteen seventy-five was the year McDuffie first came to Roycroft. "Fate and a bad marriage left me here," she recalls. A graduate of the University of Buffalo, she was teaching English and hating it when she found herself living in a remote cabin with no facilities, no money, and no support system. She had taken a ten-week potting course at a community art center and in doing so experienced a feeling of instant recognition—that she had done it before. She built her own wheel and spent two years doing nothing but shaping clay, then throwing it back in the bin. Eventually she made a gift for a friend, who in turn showed it to Bill Todorof. Todorof had established a pottery studio in an abandoned building that happened to be the original furniture-and-leather shop of the Roycroft campus. McDuffie became his apprentice in 1975; when he had financial difficulties in 1978, she borrowed $1,500 from her mother and bought the business.

Initially, she wasn't that aware of the man who was Roycroft. Elbert Hubbart was responsible for the conversion of thousands of Americans to the Arts & Crafts lifestyle and exposed millions of Americans to the movement's tenets espousing the beauty of a simple life and the spiritual rewards of honest work. Although Hubbard had been a household name until he went down with a flourish on the *Lusitania* in 1915, by the seventies, the Arts & Crafts movement had been moribund for decades.

Eventually the place—and the spirit of the larger-than-life character who employed a community of 500 artisans, published magazines read by hundreds of thousands, and built an inn just to house the seekers who came to him from all over the world—exerted its effect on McDuffie and her pottery. Bob

Rust and Kitty Turgeon-Rust as well played no small part in her learning process. Leading authorities on all things Roycroft—having led the drive to preserve the Roycroft buildings, and as authors of the current Roycroft Renaissance—the Rusts have been instrumental in the course of McDuffie's work. "They just never stopped talking Roycroft," McDuffie says gratefully. "If we didn't have them, we'd have to invent them."

Despite the Rusts' proselytizing, it was not until a trip to England in early 1990 that McDuffie's eyes were fully opened to Roycroft's role in what was undoubtedly a major international movement. It was then that she embarked on the two-year, one-hundred-test artistic odyssey that would

result in the glaze that is now signature Roycroft. There are three other glazes: Hamada Green, a moss-green tonality with pebbled surface; Tomato Glaze, evoking the rich hammered copper of Roycroft's original metalwork; and Beetlejuice Glaze, which results in a dramatic range of colors from deep green to brilliant red.

Janice McDuffie may be a master artisan, but she still holds her breath every time she opens the kiln door to a newly fired batch of pots. The fundamental elements—earth, fire, water—are always unpredictable. Over the decades, though, the artisan becomes increasingly attuned to the medium. "These days we have very few disasters," she says, "and we've never burned the building down."

Three trapezoidal vases embellished with McDuffie's glaze evokes the warmth and texture of hand-hammered copper.

Photograph © Deborah More.

Photograph © Grant Kessler.

Motawi tiles in an Arts & Crafts green make up the backsplash of this contemporary kitchen.

Nawal and Karim Motawi

Arts & Crafts Tile

Nawal Motawi began thinking of herself as an artist from the time she was in seventh grade. "I remember it well, getting interested and getting into it right away. I took art classes from that day on, always." She enjoyed prestige as the class artist of her small Michigan high school, and went straight on to the University of Michigan's School of Art, where she studied drawing and painting. Imagine her chagrin, then, when she found herself surrounded by high-quality teachers and enthusiastic students, only to realize that either fine art wasn't speaking to her or she didn't like what she was hearing. "I stuck with it a year and a half, but I was very disenchanted," she says. "I perceived the fine visual arts as phony and elitist."

She dropped out to pursue outdoor education as a vocation, but that didn't seem to be leading anywhere. By the time she returned to Michigan, she had decided that functional crafts like ceramics and weaving would be much more rewarding. Her passion for ceramics emerged that first summer semester, when a professor she greatly admired took the students on field trips to see tile installations.

"We went to see the Detroit 'People Mover' walls; this was in 1987 and they had been installed as part of the Detroit Renaissance. Pewabic Tile had done a huge one, forty by forty or more, alongside an escalator in a subway station. I just thought it was an amazingly wonderful thing to do." Motawi finished out her two years in ceramics and figure sculpture, secretly nursing the hope that one day she would get a chance to oversee the installation of one of her own major works.

Few ceramics majors in Ann Arbor would have graduated without being aware of nearby Pewabic Tile, the venerable institution founded by Mary Chase Perry Stratton in 1903 during the original Arts & Crafts movement; it is still in operation today as a business, school, museum, and gallery. Soon after graduating in the spring of 1988, Motawi landed a job there. While she realized she was lucky to be employed in the field of her choice, she discovered an ironic twist. "Tile making is actually very redundant. You think you're going to do these wonderful things, and actually what you do is stamp out tile."

Motawi worked in production, doing pressing and some glazing, before accepting a job in the bookkeeping department. She now regrets turning down a full-time job in the glazing department, but at the time she was also working part-time for an artist, volunteering at the university in exchange for studio time—and trying to do her own work. "I was

Photograph courtesy the artist.

Artist Nawal Motawi started making her own tiles while working at the venerable Pewabic Tile in Detroit. Her brother Karim joined her when production took off.

working six days a week, and volunteering, and trying to make art," she laughs. "I was making really terrible work."

But the time at Pewabic was a great experience, and a privilege, Motawi says. She stayed for four years. "It was fabulous to be involved with such a historic pottery. I was really thrilled. They're very generous there. The staff could take classes for free. They had tables in the basement so the staff could make their own work and put it at the bottom of the kilns. When I worked in bookkeeping I had a studio in the basement and really started to get into my own work. They even let me use whole kilns a couple of times when I managed to get a job."

Motawi couldn't envision a likely career path at Pewabic—she certainly wasn't cut out to be an accountant—but the idea of starting her own pottery was slow to take hold. At first she threw pots, but then "I began to see I could do tile, too. I had ideas of my own." During a residency at Detroit's Center for Creative Studies, she started to execute some of her ideas in tile, and contemplated entering a master's program in ceramic production in England. "I looked seriously at that, but my financial backers (my parents), said if this was what I really wanted to do, they would be interested in investing in a business."

In late 1991, she bought a house, rented several of the rooms to friends to pay the

Photograph courtesy the artist.

Photograph courtesy the artist.

Above, right
An assortment of Motawi tiles shows off the artistry of their designs and the luster of their glazes.

Photograph courtesy the artist.

mortgage, installed a kiln in the detached garage, and set to work. At first she remained part-time at Pewabic, hitting craft shows and art fairs on the weekends with her wares, mainly tile Christmas-tree ornaments and individual tiles with notches on the back that could be displayed on walls. She displayed some panels of tile, too, because, she says, "I knew I could do installations. I just didn't have a job to do them."

A year later, Karim, one of the youngest of Motawi's four siblings, finished college and started working with her. "Soon it became a 'we,' not just a 'me.' " Karim, fresh out of the University of Michigan with an English degree, knew nothing about ceramics, he admits. "But I always had projects and was always happiest when I was building something. Back then I just didn't know what ceramics was, but I've grown into it. Now, whether it's building an enterprise or making a tile, those are the things I find most enjoyable."

The Motawis installed their first fireplace surround at the end of 1992, but it wasn't until the next spring that their business started gaining momentum. "We were very much struggling. I didn't know how the business was going to go, but I knew I had to get some credibility. We'd started showing at the farmers' market and got a kitchen job for a client who had already done a job with Pewabic. Trust wasn't much of an issue; she understood art tile and believed it could be done. Then we installed a fireplace for a lady who had art tile in her house, then that person's neighbor decided to order her own fireplace, then their builder said, 'Oh, I'll have one of those, too.' "

Soon after, Nawal sent information on Motawi Tileworks to the Tile Heritage Foundation in California and was almost immediately contacted by Mission Tile West,

a tile showroom in Pasadena. Now Motawi tile is shown in specialty tile showrooms around the country and is a regular presence at the Grove Park Inn Arts & Crafts Conference and the International Tile and Stone Expo. Motawi tiles grace fireplace surrounds, kitchen backsplashes, and murals from the Kalamazoo Public Library to Nantucket. The business has outgrown its garage and employs three in the studio-workshop. Nawal does all the design work—designing new tiles, working with clients on drawings for installations, sculpting the tiles from which production molds are made—plus administration and marketing. Karim is the production manager ("He used to *be* production," Nawal laughs) and mold-maker. He also hand-glazes all the single-color tiles himself. "I haven't let go of that yet." Nawal and Karim have both been teaching ceramics in the community since 1993, and have even seen some of their students go on to open potteries of their own.

Although they now use a hydraulic press to pack the clay in the molds, which allows them to take on bigger jobs, there is still much handwork done on each piece of tile, particularly in the glazing. Single-color tiles get dipped rather than sprayed, Nawal explains. "Although it's a lot less efficient, it yields more aesthetically pleasing results." The polychrome tiles are colored by hand with the use of a bulb syringe, the colored glazes being meticulously applied between the raised lines of the design. In their Arts & Crafts-influenced Landscape pattern, for instance, which is designed to repeat indefinitely, the trees, bushes, and background call for five or six different colors on each tile.

They spend a lot of time developing and perfecting their glazes. "We want the glaze to do interesting things, but we don't want the tiles to vary too much or they'll look bad together.

You have to control it. But," Nawal adds, "we go to a lot of trouble to make people understand that they're buying many colors when they buy one color."

Despite the fact that most of their tile is not destined for bungalows, Motawi Tileworks remains firmly rooted in the Arts & Crafts aesthetic. "That has a lot to do with Pewabic," Nawal says. "That's where my tile aesthetic was born. The more I looked at the style, the more I liked it, especially houses and furniture. I'm interested in the spiritual and theoretical side of it, too. I love the fact that we're making something functional. For us, the saying 'Don't have anything that's not useful and beautiful' is worth adhering to."

Jerome Venneman
One-of-a-Kind Pots

Jerome Venneman leads a double life: a computer programmer for the University of California at San Francisco by day, he spends his evenings and weekends engaged in an ancient craft.

Shaping clay by hand for firing is a tradition that goes back centuries. It reached a design apotheosis in the Arts & Crafts movement through the work of such pottery communities as Rookwood, Grueby, and Teco. Pottery brought the beneficial effects of craftsmanship to the masses, too, by reaching out to the vast middle class (especially women) with workshops for the novice offered around the country. Styles incorporated an array of shapes—although most were classic—and endless variations through incised patterns, carved appliqués of animals or plants, and distinctive glazes. Arts & Crafts-movement pottery also reflected the sometimes close relationship to Art Nouveau; much of what we consider Arts & Crafts pottery wanders far from the path of honest straightforwardness espoused by the movement's founders.

Taking his stylistic clue directly from the movement's founding tenets, Jerome Venneman's pottery exemplifies beauty through simplicity. The shapes are classic, with pleasing, generally timeless, proportions. His color palette includes earthy greens and blues, and ranges from Sierra Gold to Italian Leather, with the glazes embodying a depth and texture that take on an added dimension the longer the viewer regards them. For subtle interest, he usually uses a contrasting or complementary glaze for the inside, and brings it up and over the lip of the vessel so that it edges around the rim. "It gives a visual ending for the vase from the bottom to the top, and it leads the eye from the outside to the inside," explains the artist. "I like to have the inside be on equal par with the outside."

Venneman's incised designs—all original except for his adaptation of the ubiquitous Arts & Crafts stylized rose—add interest while enhancing the stately symmetry of each piece. Like his Arts & Crafts forebears, Venneman takes his inspiration from nature: the eucalyptus tree, the sunflower, the holly bush; in deference to his passion for southwestern design, he employs stylized interpretations of arrowheads, thunderstorms, and design motifs of the ancient southwestern Pueblo cultures.

Venneman had a decade's experience as an art-pottery collector before he ever threw his first pot. This allowed ample time for the design aesthetics of the styles he most appreciated to be fully absorbed and transformed into the artist's own unique expression. It was in the early 1970s while rummaging through a San Francisco antique shop that a piece of pottery caught his eye. It appeared to be Art Nouveau, but the proprietress informed him it was a 1910 piece by Rookwood, probably the best-known pottery of the Arts & Crafts movement. It was the first time he had heard the term. Venneman struck up a friendship

with the shop owner, whose own zeal for Arts & Crafts was a great resource. He soon became passionate about the movement too, especially its pottery.

"I became an avid art-pottery collector," he recalls. "At first I was buying Rookwood production pieces and would trade up to artist-signed Rookwood pieces. Then I became interested in the Arts & Crafts period, which, at that point, was just starting to be known. There were very few books on the subject and the auctions were mostly back East. I started finding pieces for an eastern auctioneer. He would give me a finder's fee,

Venneman hand-incises his original designs—inspired by the Arts & Crafts movement and Native American tribes of the Southwest—on his signature pots, as in this version of "Whirlwind."

Photograph courtesy the artist.

Jerome Venneman's pottery exemplifies beauty through simplicity with classic shapes, pleasing proportions, and a color palette that includes earthy greens and blues, and ranges from Sierra Gold to Italian Leather. For added interest, he usually uses a complementary glaze for the inside, bringing it up and over the lip of the vessel so that it edges around the rim.

and I would amass the credits in an account with him until there was a piece I wanted to buy. I was doing this for ten years before finally deciding to take a course in pottery myself because I felt such an affinity for that particular 'art in craft'."

Perhaps it was the sudden dearth of pottery in his own home that prompted him; he had just sold his collection in order to complete the purchase of a house. His first pottery

class was at City College, and he repeated the class until they kicked him out for taking it too many times. He then went across the bridge to Marin and took an evening pottery course at a college there several times. In 1985 he traveled to Canada for a two-week course with noted ceramicist and author Robin Hopper to study microcrystalline glazes. "I was still a neophyte in terms of throwing pottery," he admits. "I really can't see how I got into the class. Hopper was a collector too, so I guess he figured I knew enough to be able to say where I wanted to go." Hopper put fifteen students through a series of extensive trials "so we'd start to understand what would happen when you put two different minerals together, whether they'd turn out matte, shiny, crystalline . . . or awful."

Back at the College of Marin, Venneman was progressing too quickly. "The facilities were very good," he explains, "but by then I was doing my own glazes and was far beyond what the instructor was doing. They wanted me to follow along with the class; I wanted to do my own thing. The instructor finally said, probably to my own betterment, 'You should go on your own now, because that's what you want to do.' "

In 1989, Venneman installed his own kiln in the basement. He spent the next six years refining his design aesthetic. "I was doing a lot of work but not design work, just using various glazes in the Fulper manner, glaze on glaze. I got tired of that and sat down to draw. It seemed natural that the designs that were coming out were obviously influenced by Arts & Crafts. I started incising pots with these designs, but the problem was most of my glazes were microcrystalline. This meant they were very fluid and didn't work well with incised pottery. So I had to develop glazes that would work well with the incised work. This meant going back to matte glazes—which, of course, worked well with Arts & Crafts."

Venneman spent two years developing his palette of glazes. "As soon as I got a couple of glazes that worked well, everything just fell together. It was the first time I felt I had something worth selling. Before that I had been giving it away."

In rapid succession, Venneman had his work picked up by two Arts & Crafts galleries in

Photograph © 1999 Chase Reynolds Ewald.

the Bay Area, and was accepted to exhibit at an Arts & Crafts show in Seattle (now defunct) and the annual Grove Park Inn Arts & Crafts Conference. Venneman's first catalog, hand printed by the Arts & Crafts Press in Berkeley, was sent out in the fall of 1997.

"As a result of all that, I suddenly had two jobs," notes Venneman, who had to cancel plans to attend a recent show because of too many orders. "This one is far more important, but for now I still need my other job because, as much as possible, I want the pottery to remain fun. Each piece is thrown to order; I wouldn't want to feel like a production potter. Within the context of people ordering from a catalog, I'm still trying to make each pot one of a kind."

So by night Jerome Venneman can be found working in the glassed-in sleeping porch of his home, surrounded by cats and classical music, Arts & Crafts furniture, his partner's oil paintings, and the beginnings of a new pottery collection. There, into the wee hours of the night, he turns out one-of-a-kind pots, one at a time.

Potter Jerome Venneman collected Arts & Crafts pottery for a decade before he ever threw a pot, then spent six years refining his design aesthetic and two years developing the unique glazes he works with today.

75

AiM HiGH & CONSiDER YOURSELF CAPABLE OF GREAT THINGS

76

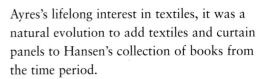

Dianne Ayres

Stylized Nature Motifs

Unlike the products of her contemporary craftsman colleagues, the work of Dianne Ayres doesn't have to compete with Arts & Crafts antiques. For, unlike a 100-year-old Morris chair, a century-old table runner—if it's even in a condition to be admired—must be stored carefully as a valuable artifact, not subjected to everyday use as originally intended.

"It's nearly impossible to decorate with antique textiles," explains Ayres, who makes pillows, table runners, and curtains and sells needlework kits to customers across the country. "Even with pieces that look pristine, the fibers are brittle and break down quickly."

Ayres would know. She was involved in textile work even as a child; her grandmother was a professional seamstress, and Ayres grew up playing and working in her sewing shop. She went on to study textile design at Indiana University before moving to Berkeley, California on the theory it was a better place to continue her studies. Still, she didn't begin making Arts & Crafts textiles until after she and her husband, Tim Hansen, had been collecting them for some time.

When they met in 1985, Hansen was already zealous about the Arts & Crafts movement, collecting period books and immersing himself in the study and historic preservation of Berkeley's architecture, much of it Arts & Crafts. As he and Ayres started spending time together, their dates often revolved around the local flea-market schedule, where they would go together in search of treasures. Given

Ayres's lifelong interest in textiles, it was a natural evolution to add textiles and curtain panels to Hansen's collection of books from the time period.

It didn't take Ayres long to notice several factors that prompted her to create her own Arts & Crafts works and offer them for sale. Antique textiles were rare and generally in a state of disintegration; many original pieces, such as those from Stickley's Craftsman Workshop, were made of jute, which breaks down quickly. Antique textiles that were still in decent condition had, in most cases, been made by amateurs from the kits popular at the time.

Ultimately, she recalls, "I realized people were not only collecting furniture but trying to live in the style." To her it was evident that textiles constituted an essential backdrop to the American interpretation of the Arts & Crafts philosophy. In creating a relaxing, nurturing, nature-related environment, turn-of-the-century housewives had been advised by Gustav Stickley's *Craftsman*, as well as leading women's magazines such as *Ladies' Home Journal* and *House Beautiful*, that they could add warmth, color, and texture to their homes through the use of textiles. Runners lessened the severity of the plain tables, and pillows softened the hard edges of chairs and settles; portieres (curtains hung in open doorways) replaced heavy, impenetrable doors with lightweight fabric that offered privacy while hinting at intimacy.

Because Craftsman-style linens were light in weight and sparely embellished, they could be

Facing
Aphorism, exhortation, and pithy sayings were common motifs in Arts & Crafts decorating. They appear in the Revival on textiles—as on this motto panel—and carved over doorways or into mantels.

added to an interior without resulting in the heavy, cluttered, overly ornamented look typical of the fading Victorian period against which the movement was a reaction. Nature was brought indoors through stylized designs of pinecones, ginkgo leaves, seedpods, roses, and the lotus. "An atmosphere of restfulness, friendliness, and comfort was to be achieved by the thoughtful application of the fundamentals of the arrangement of space and the right use of color and texture," Ayres writes in *Arts and Crafts Quarterly*. "Textiles, such as table runners, curtains and pillows, formed an integral component of the Craftsman home scheme."

Ayres was still a student at U.C. Berkeley at the time, and would graduate with a B.A. in conservation and resource studies. "I know it sounds unrelated [to textile design]—it was

Photograph © 1999 Chase Reynolds Ewald.

mostly plant studies," she says, "but it was very helpful in learning to identify plants and also understanding how fibers are made." She was contemplating getting a "real job" when she started researching her newfound interest instead. "I was in the U.C. Berkeley library, reading *Craftsman* magazines, *Ladies' Home Journals*, and other design books of the time period to see what Arts & Crafts textiles really were.

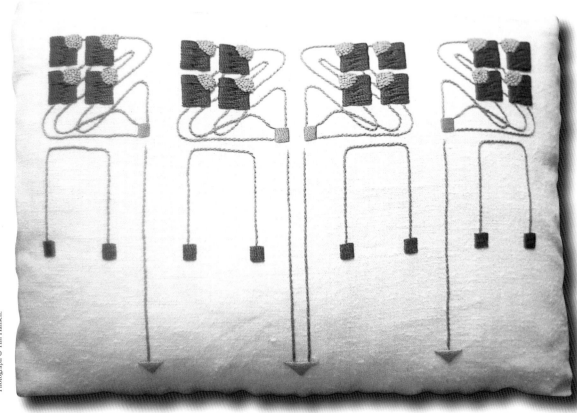

Photograph © Tim Hansen.

"Those first years were like an apprenticeship to the Arts & Crafts movement," she recalls. And at first, she was solely reproducing designs from the original movement, mainly those from Gustav Stickley's workshops. Ayres's stylized lotus, checkerberry, ginkgo, and pinecone motifs, for instance, come courtesy of the Craftsman Workshops. Other perennial favorites include the Roycroft Rose, which places appliqués of stylized, paprika-colored flowers and green leaves above hand-embroidered brown stems; three gold squares, hand embroidered one above the other between the two flowers, add a hint of Scottish designer Charles Rennie Mackintosh. Another Roycroft design is adapted from a stained-glass window by Dard Hunter.

In recent years, though, Ayres has increasingly found herself working from her own original designs. Her gold-rendered poppy design, a stylized version of California's state flower, is something Stickley himself might have come up with had he spent a spring in California. She works closely with clients on one-of-a-kind custom projects too. Ayres has replaced the textiles for such Arts & Crafts meccas as Stickley's Craftsman Farms and the Thorsen House in Berkeley. In the spirit of Gustav Stickley's promotion of do-it-yourselfness, Ayres's Arts & Crafts Period Textiles also offers twenty-five different kits, "partly to make the textiles more affordable, and partly because that's what was being done at the time. I've found it a really rewarding aspect of the work. People call and tell me how much they love doing it; people send me photos of their grandmothers surrounded by pillows they've made."

The rapid growth of her endeavor caught Ayres by surprise, she admits. "When I first started out, I thought I would sit around the fire at night and do embroidery. But it soon became apparent that there wasn't enough time." She now has several employees to help with the embroidery and appliqué work. She does all the design work, collaborates with clients on custom orders, and spends more time than she would like on paperwork. (Some days she wishes the phone wouldn't ring) Annual Arts & Crafts events in Pasadena, San Francisco, and at the Grove Park Inn have become "like old-home week," the places where she keeps in touch with regular customers and meets new ones.

"I love to make things with my hands, but I don't like to have a lot of stuff around. It's nice to make things but not keep it all, not get bogged down by all the possessions." At the same time, she realizes, "I'm pretty fortunate to be able to do what I love."

Ann Wallace & Friends
Custom-designed Textiles

The fact that Ann Wallace's life is defined by Arts & Crafts is the result of a series of fortuitous circumstances ranging from a lifelong interest in handwork and textiles to her husband's job transfer, which landed her right in the middle of a community of Prairie School bungalows. It was also inevitable, because she had a family history with the style and because she personally embraces so many basics tenets of the movement's philosophy.

"I'm a natural-born dilettante," says the craftsman. So when a close friend and neighbor appeared on her doorstep, frantic because his Arts & Crafts home would soon be featured on a major house tour and he had just realized he had no window coverings, Wallace impulsively committed to making the curtains. For the entire house. In the appropriate style. And it gave shape to her life's work, weaving all the seemingly disparate strands

Ann Wallace's designs—executed
in rich embroidery—take their cues
from nature.

together into a pattern that made the most perfect sense.

Wallace grew up in New York City, "not the place you think of someone growing up sewing at their mother's knee—although my mother did sew. She made wonderful doll clothes and fabulous Halloween costumes. My father's mother lived in Spokane, Washington, and made beautiful quilts; she was always winning blue ribbons at the state fair. There were always lots of clay and fabric and paper dolls and things to cut up around the house."

In addition to the arts and crafts ("with a small a and c," she says) influence, Wallace also had the Arts & Crafts influence through her maternal grandmother. "She was an avid follower of Roycroft. She went to college with the famous illegitimate daughter of Elbert Hubbard; she wrote her honors thesis on the influence of the Roycroft movement. Her home was filled with Roycroft furniture. When we cleaned her house after she died, we found five different versions of [Elbert Hubbard's] *The Little Journeys*. It was a major interest of hers—almost like a cult. And this was during the slump in interest in Arts & Crafts nationwide."

As an undergraduate at Oberlin College, Wallace was always interested in textiles. "If I was taking a course on impressionism, I would write the paper on how a particular artist would render textiles," she recalls. She spent a lot of time doing theater work, usually making costumes, "always by the seat of my pants."

She went on to receive an M.F.A in theater design from Carnegie Mellon University, then went to Boston, where she remained for fifteen years, teaching and doing theater design. "It was a wonderful way to be exposed to a whole lot of different things: fabric painting, embroidery, sourcing. I learned how to get things done. I wasn't just sitting around doing airy-fairy stuff." During this time she married, and in 1984 her husband, a television and film producer, was offered a job at a major regional theater; hence, the move to St. Paul.

At first she thought she had landed in the hinterlands. But she soon discovered, "It's a lovely, lovely city." And full of Arts & Crafts-era neighborhoods that were intact. "The Arts & Crafts Revival, at least in terms of craftsmen, is very much centered in the West," Wallace says, "but this area was the birthplace of the Prairie School. At the turn of the century they were building a lot of wonderful Arts & Crafts buildings. On the East Coast, Arts & Crafts tends to get buried behind the Victorian and Georgian architecture. But there are tons of Frank Lloyd Wright and Sullivan buildings here. In Decatur, Illinois, there's a whole street of houses built by students of Frank Lloyd Wright. I'd been aware of Arts & Crafts, of course, especially William Morris, but not how the movement played out in the U.S. And this was a wonderful way to find it, just walking down the street. I saw all these Arts & Crafts buildings, and I just fell in love with it.

"And I loved the idea behind it," she adds. "It's so rare to fall in love with the way something looks and find this philosophy behind it. It still works here in the Midwest. There's a strong Scandinavian frugality here, and people are interested in reviving neighborhoods and bringing communities together and living a spiritually fulfilling and less materialistic lifestyle—rather than just collecting expensive lamps. There's a unique twist on the Arts & Crafts movement here, a Prairie twist on things that's different from, say, the Arroyo twist." (The Arroyo area in Pasadena holds a number of Greene & Greene residences.) It's ironic, she says, but "I would never have noticed Arts & Crafts if I had stayed on the East Coast."

Wallace and her husband bought a bungalow within a year of moving and set about to restore it. "It was very difficult to find stuff," she recalls. "A lot of the things we needed were not out there, and a lot of information too. How do you clean stained-glass windows, for instance? We definitely had to dig. But also we could walk around the neighborhood and see houses that hadn't been changed, and we could see what was there. Of course, some had been trashed, but those that are left are now considered treasures."

Wallace and her husband restored that house, living there for six years before the need for more space pushed them to buy another Arts & Crafts house, built in 1908, which Wallace describes as "transitional; Prairie style without all the horizontal lines."

Wallace had taken a job as advertising director for a Swiss sewing-machine manufacturing company, and although she stayed six years, she was on the lookout for something that would speak more to her sensibilities. That was when her neighbor proposed she make the curtains for his home. If it hadn't been for a phone call with her sister the night before the house tour, Wallace would have neglected to put out business cards. As it was, she did—and got two calls immediately.

The house tour was in the fall of 1992, Wallace quit her job in January of 1993, and her business has been in the black ever since. Custom-designed curtains have always been the biggest percentage of her business; pillows and runners were added more recently. She also sells kits. "They're a really small part of what I do," she says, "but I'll always sell things like that because it's therapeutic for people who want to do things with their hands."

Much of what Wallace does involves custom design work, which she really enjoys. "I look at lots and lots of graphic arts books, then I put them aside and start drawing, and I come up with something that's my own design but still Arts & Crafts. I get a lot of inspiration from the garden, too. My Italian husband is the gardener—and I'm the appreciative audience."

Because of her long years of theatrical work, Wallace works fast. She creates using a mixture of watercolor, gouache, and magic marker, and sometimes colored pencil as well. "The best designs," she says, "have an elegance about them."

Wallace's fabric of choice is linen, but finding a dependable source is a constant effort. "The textile market is very international and highly third world." The U.S., she says, doesn't have the right climate for linen production, and the countries producing linen—Belgium, Ireland, India, eastern Europe—are inconsistent suppliers due to politics and weather fluctuations. To make matters worse, when an importer becomes successful, they no longer want to fill the smaller orders Wallace's business represents. Consequently, she spends a great deal of time traveling to trade shows. "I'm constantly looking, all the time."

The designs—some Stickley- and Roycroft-influenced, but most of them decidedly her own—are rendered on fabric through a

A textile expert and theater designer, Ann Wallace grew up influenced by arts and crafts around the home and Arts & Crafts through her grandmother, an avid follower of all things Roycroft.

Ann Wallace & Friends' meticulous embroidery on natural linens maintains the simple, clean look of this bungalow while softening the severe lines of Arts & Crafts woodwork.

combination of embroidery, appliqué, and stenciling, using a water-based textile paint. (When it comes to paint, she has no qualms about embracing modern technology. "I have old recipe books for making textile paints using gasoline and pigment. This stuff was terrifying! At least now you don't have to worry about setting your house on fire.")

The "friends" in Ann Wallace & Friends consist of six women who sew for her, mostly out of their own homes, but Wallace is not content to merely design; she still does plenty of needlework.

"My goal," she says, "was to *not* get out of the workroom." And with custom jobs and tight deadlines, there's always a good reason to sit down and embroider.

Ironically, Wallace points out, "sewing is not so therapeutic when you're working against a deadline. For relaxation," she says, "I knit."

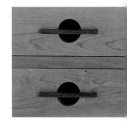

Furniture

Photograph © Greg Krogstad.

Facing
Thomas Hugh Stangeland teams modified Greene & Greene dining chairs with a mortise-and-through-tenon table of contemporary styling.

Top
The Greene & Greene spirit is in the details, as in the corner of a desk by Thomas Hugh Stangeland.

Bottom
A server by Tom Stangeland combines an Arts & Crafts form with lustrous wood, hand-wrought hardware, and ebony peg details.

Photograph © Greg Krogstad.

Right
A streamlined writing desk from M. T. Maxwell Furniture Company shows an Arts & Crafts spirit.

Photograph courtesy the artist.

Below
The influence of Greene & Greene is apparent in the work of Stangeland through his use of the cloud-lift motif and beautiful inlay work

Photograph © Greg Krogstad.

Thomas Hugh Stangeland's Arts &
Crafts aesthetic is both unique and
contemporary.

Warren Hile designed his first piece of furniture after he restored a 1921 California bungalow, then had difficulty finding appropriate furnishings. His spindle-backed settle and chairs fit perfectly in any period bungalow.

Photograph © Alex Vertikoff, courtesy Warren Hile Studio.

Warren Hile addresses the contemporary needs of the Revival period in the design of this computer desk.

Above
The lighter design and high foot- and headboard of this spindle bed lend a contemporary feel to this piece from Warren Hile Studio.

Right
Thomas Hugh Stangeland's glass-topped Arts & Crafts table is decidedly contemporary.

Photograph © 1999 Chase Reynolds Ewald.

Below
Mortise and through-tenon and spindles are hallmarks of Arts & Crafts design, as seen in this dining suite from Stickley.

Above
Thomas Starbuck Stockton's Greene & Greene-inspired dining chairs add elegance to a light-filled home overlooking San Francisco Bay.

Facing
Craftsman Raymond Tillman's work is unique—inspired by the Arts & Crafts movement but combining a range of influences. His deacon seat/storage bench bears cast-bronze seascape panels and the four-square cutout motif favored by Charles Rennie Mackintosh.

Left
Round Valley Iron & Woodworks' Arts & Crafts furniture is both contemporary and western.

Right
A Stickley-esque cabinet piece from Warren Hile Studio features heavy strap hinges made by craftsman Chris Efker.

Below
Architect John Kelly has been designing Arts & Crafts-influenced furniture for a decade. Like all the pieces in his J1 line, this double drawer box, an accessory piece indended to rest atop a bureau or desk, is of solid cherry with walnut pegs and features Kelly's distictive drawer pulls.

Photograph © Alex Vertikoff, courtesy Warren Hile Studio.

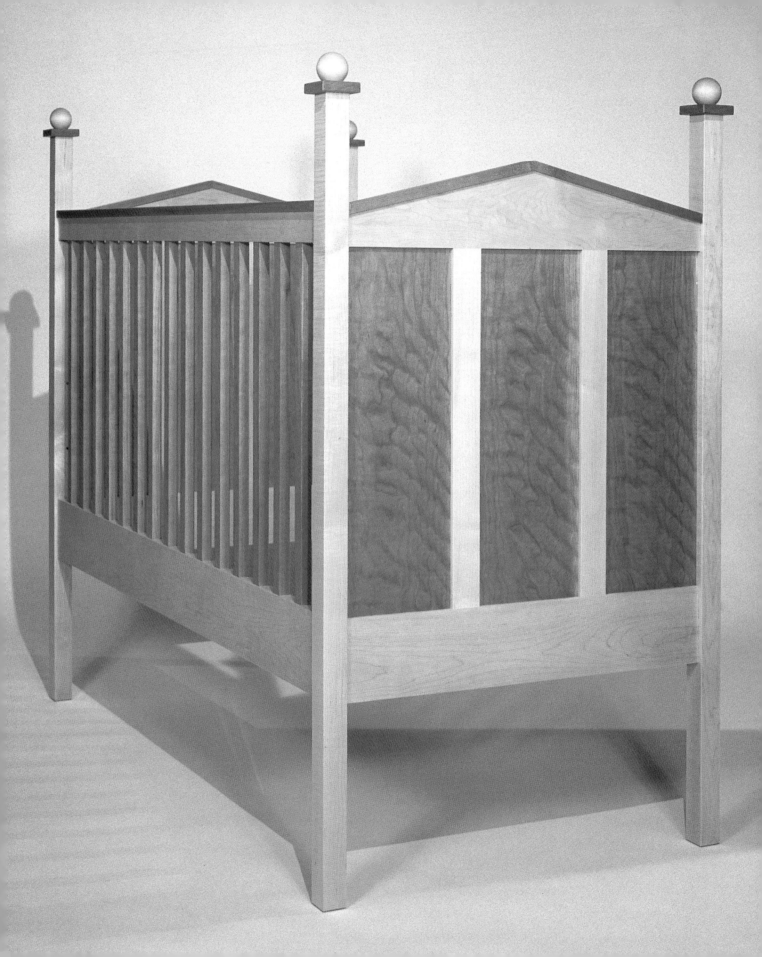

Left
An unusual crib from M. T. Maxwell combines Arts & Crafts with Greek Revival.

Right
M. T. Maxwell's spindle chair lightens and makes contemporary an Arts & Crafts classic.

M. T. Maxwell's Arts & Crafts
furniture pursues the Asian
aesthetic, as in the distinctive
drawer pulls of this cabinet.

Tom Stockton designed these
massive Arts & Crafts chairs for
this windy pool-side setting in
the hills of Sausalito.

Photograph courtesy the artist.

Photograph courtesy the artist.

Above
A junkyard-inspired Arts & Crafts side chair by Whit McLeod combines previously used Douglas fir, plywood, nails, and hemp.

Left
David Berman's "Voysey Bed I" is of quartered oak posts with a distinctive Voysey motif: square posts tapering upward to octagons.

Facing
Molesworth meets Mission in this Arts & Crafts chair, ottoman, and side table from New West.

Left
Whit McLeod uses recycled redwood for this sturdy Arts & Crafts bench.

Below
John Kelly's award-winning daybed, of solid cherry with walnut pegs and pulls, has wedged tenons on the armrests and a wood-on-wood drawer slide design that allows the drawers to open in both directions.

Craftsman David Berman looks to Europe for his inspiration, as in this reinterpretation of the richly handpainted "Butterfly Cabinet" by E. W. Godwin (the original painted by Whistler), adapted here for media use.

Above
A secretary desk from M. T. Maxwell Furniture Company shows a strong Asian aesthetic.

Left
David Hellman works almost exclusively in the style of architect brothers Greene & Greene, as seen in this mahogany and ebony hall table.

Ted Scherrer gives a contemporary
look to his bow-arm Morris chair.

A Greene & Greene-inspired stand-up writing desk of Honduran mahogany is from Good Life Artisans and Designers.

Facing
Paul Pacak shows his fascination with Frank Lloyd Wright in this unusual writing desk.

Above
This cabinet, richly painted and stenciled, was adapted by David Berman from a 1858 design by William Burges, who, Berman says, was "a medieval fantasy architect."

Nielsen Woodworks' signature piece is this mahogany-and-ebony occasional table with marble insert, inspired by Greene & Greene's Fern table, designed for the Gamble House.

John Welch's all-copper hand-hammered floor lamp with mica shade casts a warm glow.

Lighting

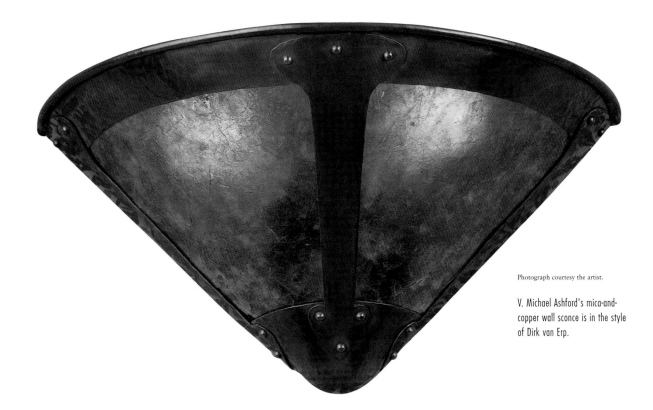

Photograph courtesy the artist.

V. Michael Ashford's mica-and-copper wall sconce is in the style of Dirk van Erp.

Photograph courtesy the artist.

A five-pendant chandelier from V. Michael Ashford of mica and copper has medieval overtones.

New York craftsman Raymond Tillman has been working in the Arts & Crafts style for a decade. His lamp shows the Celtic influence that is a hallmark of his style.

Photograph courtesy the artist.

Below
Designer Kip Mesirow's copper lighting fixtures appear throughout the world-famous Chez Panisse Restaurant in Berkeley, California.

Photograph © 1999 Chase Reynolds Ewald.

Four Stickley-style pendants with soft yellow opalescent glass hang from John Welch's copper chandelier. The body of the piece features three nickel-silver squares on each quadrant, while the chains are handmade of copper.

Walls

Trimbelle River Studio's
"Kuai" stencil brightens this
bungalow nook.

The Apple Tree frieze from Bradbury
& Bradbury creates a formal,
potentially endlessly repeating pattern from a stylized image taken
from the natural world.

The "Sanctuary" stencil from
Trimbelle River Studios features an
infinitely repeating stylized design
in muted Arts & Crafts colors.

Bradbury & Bradbury's Art
Wallpapers, like this Springfield
stripe paired with the Arcadia border, are hand-printed at their
workshop in northern California.

Photograph © Bruce Smith.

A stencil by Helen Foster adds color and a touch of elegance to an Arts & Crafts dining room.

Photograph courtesy the artist.

Helen Foster's stencils, featuring stylized images usually derived from nature, add an Arts & Crafts period touch to any contemporary home, as is the case with her "Pendant" design.

Half-curtains, by Ann Wallace &
Friends, soften the hard lines of the
Arts & Crafts bungalow.

Ceramics

Ceramics by David Ross feature classic forms and unusual glazing techniques.

Photograph courtesy the artist.

David Ross has perfected the Arts & Crafts green for his distinctive pottery.

Photograph courtesy the artist.

Ceramicist Stuart Compton offers Arts & Crafts bookends as well as hand-made tiles.

Left
Fulper Tile was part of the original Arts & Crafts movement. Its participation in the revival came when Fulper's granddaughters found the secret glaze formulas in the attic. Today the company produces custom tiles, as for this home's handpainted frieze.

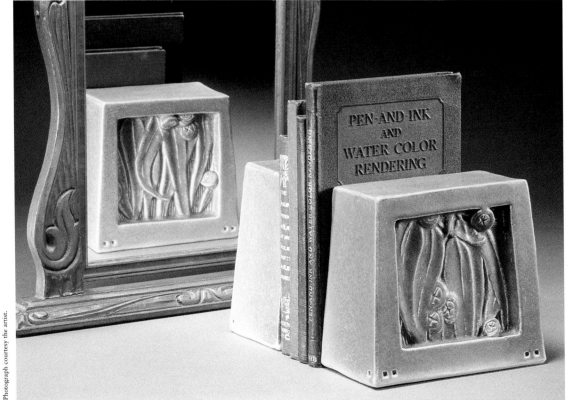

PEN-AND-INK AND WATER COLOR RENDERING

Photograph courtesy the artist.

Accessories

Facing
The spirit of the plains is evident in this Arts & Crafts-inspired piece from Round Valley Iron & Woodworks in Montana.

Above
Copperwork by John Welch— poppy candlesticks, a camelia bowl, clock, writing set, and Roycroft-inspired table lamp—pays tribute to the styles forged by Dirk van Erp, Karl Kipp, and Roycroft.

Right
The Manzanita mirror from Holton Furniture and Frame, in carved and painted Honduran mahogany, is in the turn-of-the-century California Decorative style of Arthur and Lucia Mathews.

A Holton mirror fits effortlessly
into a period bungalow.

Although copper is the more ubiquitous material used in Arts & Crafts metalwork, Laity & Miller are unusual for their work in silver, such as these Prairie candlesticks.

Above
Tim Holton's mortise-and-through-tenon frame—shown here in quartersawn white oak framing an Edward S. Curtis photogravure—is an Arts & Crafts classic.

Left
Master metalworker Audel Davis is celebrated for his work in the style of Dirk van Erp.

Photograph courtesy Thomas Reynolds Gallery.

Hand-hammered copperwork by
Audel Davis has warmth, solidity,
and a timeless quality.

Audel Davis' copperwork runs the
gamut from standing lamps to
small desktop pieces, with handwork apparent in each.

Photograph courtesy the artist.

M. T. Maxwell's furniture has a
look that is contemporary enough
for a New York brick-walled loft.

Roomscapes

Illuminating the reproduction Frank Lloyd Wright dining table and chairs is a custom piece by Dennis Casey, an inverted and enlarged version of a double-pedestal lamp designed by Wright for the 1902 Dana-Thomas House in Springfield, Illinois.

A Mission oak dining-room suite from Warren Hile Studio.

A carpet designed by David
Berman is based on C. F. A.
Voysey's "Green Pastures" design,
executed in cross-stitch. The heart-
shaped cutout in the chair is a
favorite Voysey motif.

Photograph courtesy the artist.

Historic or contemporary? Stickley's roomscape features both in pairing its furniture with stained-glass windows, a stenciled frieze, a Dirk van Erp-style lamp, and a pendant-style hanging lighting fixture.

Facing
Stickley offers modern interpretations of Arts & Crafts classics: the settle, the Morris chair, the tile-topped table (adapted here as a coffee table), and the tabouret table.

Left
Bradbury & Bradbury Art Wallpaper's Piedmont border with Springfield stripe create an elegant, formal touch to the Arts & Crafts dining room of a 1920s bungalow.

Dianne Ayres's Acorn portieres and Checkerberry pillows—the latter embroidered from the kits Ayres offers—blend seamlessly with antiques against a Bradbury & Bradbury hand-printed wallpaper.

Photograph courtesy the artist.

Hinting of Asia and the Arts & Crafts movement, M. T. Maxwell furniture works well in the non-bungalow.

Facing
A contemporary suite of bedroom furniture from Stickley lends an air of period authenticity to an Arts & Crafts room.

Above
An elaborate period stained-glass window forms the backdrop for Mack & Rodel's Harvey Ellis bookcase with hand-blown glass, flat-armed Morris chair, and Limbert book stand. The clock and table are David Berman reproductions of C. F. A. Voysey designs.

Overleaf
The living room of this Frank Lloyd Wright-inspired house combines western art with contemporary Arts & Crafts pieces: a Nielsen Woodworks table, a sconce by Dennis Casey, and a pot by Jerome Venneman.

DIRECTORY AND SOURCEBOOK

■ **The Artisans**

■ ■ *Furniture/Woodwork*

A.K.A. Drake
David B. "Drake" Adkisson
619 Western Avenue #17
Seattle, WA 98104
206-467-1761
adkisson@ix.netcom.com
*Handcrafted furniture in hardwoods
with copper repoussé and slate.*

Berkeley Mills
2830 Seventh Street
Berkeley, CA 94710
510-549-2853
www.berkeley-mills.com
*Custom manufacturer of craftsman-
style furniture.*

David Berman
Trustworth Studio
P.O. Box 1109
Plymouth, MA 02362
508-746-1847
*Arts & Crafts furniture & lighting
in the English style.*

Todd Brotherton
P.O. Box 404
Mount Shasta, CA 96067
530-938-4000
toddb@snowcrest.net
Master Furniture Maker.

Gerry Brown
Floating World Wood Design
144 Biltmore Avenue
Asheville, NC 28801
704-281-1118
gbrown@buncombe.main.nc.us
*Hand-carved doors and architectur-
al elements.*

James Byer
136 East Street, Unit E
Arcadia, CA 91006
818-445-7451
Bungalow furniture.

Century Craftsman
P.O. Box 136, RR 1
Corbeil, Ontario P0H 1K0
705-752-2296
centurycraft@efni.com
*Retail line offers reproduction
Stickley-inspired mission oak.*

Jim Dailey
Present Time Clocks
18452 Skagit City Road
Mount Vernon, WA 98273
360-445-4702
*Handmade signed-and-numbered
Craftsman clocks.*

Arnold d'Epagnier
14201 Notley Road
Colesville, MD 20904
301-384-1663
*Roycroft Master Artisan producing
twenty-first-century Arts & Crafts-
style furniture.*

Fair Haven Woodworks
Ted Scherrer
500 Larrabee Avenue
Bellingham, WA 98225

Floating World Wood Designs
144 Biltmore Avenue
Asheville, NC 28801
704-281-1118
gbrown@buncombe.main.nc.us
*Hand-carved doors and architec-
tural elements.*

Good Life Artisans and Designers
P.O. Box 41434
Bungalow Heaven, CA 91114
626-797-9098

Green Design Furniture Company
267 Commercial Street
Portland, ME 04101
1-800-853-4234
*Contemporary cherry furniture with
an Arts & Crafts feel.*

David Hellman
86 Highland Avenue
Watertown, MA 02472
617-923-4829
Greene & Greene-inspired furniture.

Warren Hile Studios
89 East Montecito Avenue
Sierra Madre, CA 91024
626-355-4382
HileStudio@aol.com
Manufacturer of Mission furniture.

Holton Furniture and Frame
5515 Doyle Street, No. 2
Emeryville, CA 94608
1-800-250-5277
Craftsman frames and mirrors.

James Ipekjian
Ipekjian Custom Woodwork
768 North Fair Oaks Avenue
Pasadena, CA 91103
626-792-5025
Greene & Greene master artisan.

Preston Jordan
P.O. Box 55
Madison, NJ 07940
Stickley furniture craftsman.

John Kelly Furniture Design
144 Chambers Street
New York, NY 10007
212-385-1885
www.johnkellyfurniture.com
*Kelly's J1 series offers innovative,
Arts & Crafts-influenced, handmade cherry furniture.*

Paul Kemner
2829 Rockwood
Toledo, OH 43610
419-241-8278
pkemner@bright.net
*Handmade Arts & Crafts reproduc-
tions and original designs, including
clocks. Kemner authored* Building
Arts & Crafts Furniture.

The Ralph Kylloe Collection
P.O. Box 669
Lake George, NY 12845
518-696-4100
*High-end rustic hickory furniture in
the Arts & Crafts tradition.*

The Lane Co., Inc.
East Franklin Avenue
Altavista, VA 24517
804-369-5641
*Furniture manufacturer offering a
"Grove Park Inn" collection.*

Mack & Rodel
44 South Leighton Road
Pownal, ME 04069
207-688-4483
www.neaguild.com/macrodel
*A husband-and-wife shop producing
fine Arts & Crafts furniture.*

M.T. Maxwell Furniture Co.
Michael T. Maxwell
715 Liberty Street
Bedford, VA 24523
1-800-686-1844
www.maxwellfurniture.com
Handcrafted hardwood furniture.

Michael McGlynn
501 First Avenue NE
Minneapolis, MN 55413
612-331-1739
*Frank Lloyd Wright-, Prairie
School-, and Greene & Greene-
inspired fine furniture.*

Craig McIlwain
Black Swamp Handcraft
3901 Chipplegate
Toldeo, OH 43614
Furniture.

Whit McLeod
P.O. Box 132
Arcata, CA 95518
707-822-7307
*Distinctive Arts & Crafts furniture
made from recycled wine barrels.*

Thos. Moser Cabinetmakers
Auburn, ME 04211
1-800-708-9703
*Manufacturer of Shaker- and Arts
& Crafts-inspired furniture.*

Cliff Nathan
4530 Beekman Avenue
Studio City, CA 91604
818-762-3113
*Woodworker making Arts & Crafts
furniture and accessories.*

Nielsen Woodworks
Doug & Jenny Nielsen
P.O. Box 2678
Arnold, CA 95223
209-795-6204
Arts & Crafts mirrors and woodwork.

Old Hickory Furniture Co.
403 South Noble Street
Shelbyville, IN 46176
1-800-232-BARK
*More than 140 hickory designs,
many from the early 1900s, including the Grove Park rocker.*

Michael Pulhalski
1526 First Avenue South
Seattle, WA 98134
206-233-9581
*Furniture maker, including Stickley
reproductions for Craftsman Farms.*

Jaap Romijn and Friends
5515 Doyle Street #17
Emeryville, CA 94608
510-652-8835
Fine furniture.

Round Valley Iron and Woodworks
Vance and Joanne Paulson
P.O. Box 3744
Bozeman, MT 59772
406-582-0929
rvalley@avicom.net
*Mission- and Prairie-inspired custom
furniture, including unusual items
like a trundle daybed, a wooden
room divider, and quilt rack.*

Ted Scherrer
Fairhaven Woodworks
500 Larrabee Avenue
Bellingham, WA 98225
360-733-3411
www.pacificrim.net/~tedscher
*Furniture maker/designer, primarily
in the Arts & Crafts style.*

Thomas Stangeland
800 Mercer Street
Seattle, WA 98109
206-622-2004
*Furniture and cabinet maker using
design language of Arts & Crafts
and Art Deco periods in contemporary work.*

Stickley Furniture
Stickley Drive, P.O. Box 480
Manlius, NY 13104
315-682-5500
*Reproductions and contemporary
interpretations of Stickley brothers
furniture.*

Thomas Starbuck Stockton
P.O. Box 38
Montgomery Creek, CA 96065
530-337-6797
starbuck@dnai.com
www.dnai.com/~starbuck
Fine custom-made furniture.

Swartzendruber Hardwood Creations
1100 Chicago Avenue
Goshen, IL 46526
1-800-531-2502
Furniture manufacturer offering a "Prairie Collection."

Raymond Tillman
9 Fairview Avenue
Chatham, NY 12037
518-392-4603
raybrin@capital.net
Furniture maker employing oak, stained glass, and bronze with Celtic motifs.

Voorhees Craftsman
P.O. Box 1938
Rohnert Park, CA 94927
707-584-5044
Arts & Crafts antiques dealers who also offer a line of custom reproductions.

Wood Classics
P.O. Box 291
Gardiner, NY 12525
914-255-7871
Arts & Crafts replica kit furniture.

Debey Zito
55 Bronte Street
San Francisco, CA 94110
415-648-6861
Meticulously handcrafted, hand-sanded, hand-rubbed, Asian-influenced Arts & Crafts furniture.

■ ■ *Metalwork*

Michael Adams
Aurora Studios
109 Main Street
Putnam, CT 06260
860-928-6662
Hand-hammered copper lamps, chandeliers.

Arts & Crafts Hardware
Gerry Rucks
28011 Malvina
Warren, MI 48093
810-772-7279
Handcrafted Arts & Crafts hardware.

Michael Ashford
6543 Alpine Drive SW
Olympia, WA 98512
360-352-0694
Hand-hammered copper and mica lamps.

Arnold Benetti
727 Baker Street
San Francisco, CA 94115
415-567-2107
Hand-hammered copper lamps and vases.

Buffalo Studios
Greg Bowman
1925 Deere Avenue
Santa Ana, CA 92705
714-250-7333
Three decades of Arts & Crafts metalwork.

Audel Davis
510-843-7071
Hand-hammered copper lamps, bookends, vases in the style of Dirk van Erp.

Chris Efker
Craftsman Hardware Co.
P.O. Box 161
Marceline, MO 64658
660-376-2481
Hand-hammered copper, brass, and bronze hardware.

Historical Arts & Casting
5580 West Bagley Park Road
West Jordan, UT 84088
1-800-225-1414
Cast reproductions of Louis H. Sullivan and Frank Lloyd Wright designs.

The Laity & Miller Co.
Robert Laity and Brian Miller
820 West End Avenue
New York, NY 10025
212-316-2150
Arts & Crafts-influenced silversmiths; handwrought copperwork.

Kip Mesirow
Verdigris Copperworks
810 Camelia
Berkeley, CA 94710
510-525-1922
Original designs in copper. Work prominently featured at the world-class Chez Panisse Restaurant.

Seattle Copper Art
P.O. Box 84944
Seattle, WA 98124-6244
206-324-1185
Hand-formed, "fire colored" copper, both replicas and original works.

John Welch
4920 Lone Lake Road
Langley, WA 98260
360-321-2293
Hammered copper inspired by Dirk van Erp and Karl Kipp.

■ ■ *Art Glass/Mica*

Dennis Casey
Prairie Designs of California
P.O. Box 886
Brisbane, CA 94005
415-468-5446
Frank Lloyd Wright-inspired and reproduction stained-glass lamps and windows.

Patricia & Guiliano Deganis
Inlight Art Glass
565 Elmwood Avenue
Buffalo, NY 14222
716-881-3564
Arts & Crafts and contemporary stained glass panels, windows, and lighting.

John S. Hamm
Hamm Glass
6310 Washington Avenue
Whittier, CA 90601
562-696-3364
Art-glass craftsman.

Judson Studios
200 South Avenue 66
Los Angeles, CA 90042
1-800-445-8376
Stained and faceted glass since 1897.

Brian McNally
3236 Calle Pinon
Santa Barbara, CA 93105
805-687-7212
Art glass, mainly lamps and windows.

Tim Merritte
115 West Calfornia Boulevard, 432
Pasadena, CA 91105
626-564-9100
Custom mica shades, leather lacing, sinew, or leaded.

Metro Lighting & Crafts
2216 San Pablo Avenue
Berkeley, CA 94702
1-888-METRO20
www.metrolighting.com
Arts & Crafts and art-nouveau lamps, reproductions and interpretations.

Mica Lamp Co.
517 State Street
Glendale, CA 91203
818-241-7227
Arts & Crafts-style lighting.

Mission Spirit
9900 West Spirit Lake Road
Spirit Lake, ID 83869-9744
1-800-433-4211
Mission lighting fixtures of quartersawn white oak and art glass or mica.

Rejuvenation Lamp & Fixture Co.
1100 SE Grand Avenue
Portland, OR 97214
888-343-8548
www.rejuvenation.com
More than 260 examples of authentic reproduction lighting: chandeliers, wall brackets, porch lights, lamps. Extensive Arts & Crafts collection.

■ ■ *Textiles*

Dianne Ayres
Arts & Crafts Period Textiles
5427 Telegraph Avenue #W2
Oakland, CA 94609
510-654-1645
ACPTextile@AOL.com
Hand-stenciled pillows, runners, tablecloths, and kits; Roycrofters-at-Large Artisan.

Liza Jennings Seiner
108 Summerhill Lane
Level Green, PA 15085
412-856-8234
Roycrofters-at-Large Artisan offering hand-stenciled, hand-sewn table linens and counted-cross-stitch kits.

Ann Wallace & Friends
767 Linwood Avenue
St. Paul, MN 55105
612-228-9611
Hand-embroidered and stenciled Arts & Crafts curtains, cushions, and table linens.

Barbara Wheat
6333 NE Mallory Avenue
Portland, OR 97211
503-286-5770
Unique etched-velvet pillows with naturalistic Arts & Crafts designs using the Devore process developed in Europe in the 1800s.

■ ■ *Pottery/Tile*

C & C Brown Potters
541-336-3668
Arts & Crafts-inspired pottery.

Stuart Compton
510-526-7356
2031 Berryman Street
Berkeley, CA 94709
Ceramicist making Arts & Crafts-style tiles, clocks, lamps, and bookends.

Ephraim Faience Pottery
P.O. Box 792
Brookfield, WI 53007
1-888-704-POTS
Contemporary Arts & Crafts pottery.

Fulper Tile
34 West Ferry Street
New Hope, PA 18938
215-862-3358
Art-tile company established in 1860, now run by granddaughters of the founder.

Janice McDuffie
Roycroft Potters
37 South Grove Street
East Aurora, NY 14052
716-652-7422
rrpotters@aol.com
Roycroft Master Artisan producing hand-thrown, high-fired porcelain vases.

Moravian Pottery and Tileworks
130 Swamp Road
Doylestown, PA 18901
215-345-6722
Historic Arts & Crafts tile manufacturer.

Motawi Tileworks
Karim & Nawal Motawi
33 North Steabler, Suite 2
Ann Arbor, MI 48103
734-213-0017
Art tile.

Pewabic Pottery
10125 East Jefferson Avenue
Detroit, MI 48214
313-822-0954
*Historic Arts & Crafts pottery, also
a museum and teaching institution.*

David Ross Ceramics
P.O. Box 1668
Sonoma, CA 95476
707-996-2192
Arts & Crafts pottery.

Tile Restoration Center, Inc.
3511 Interlake Avenue North
Seattle, WA 98103
206-633-4866
www.almnet.com/~tcolson/pages/trc/
trc.htm
Reproduction and restoration of historic tiles.

Van Briggle
600 South 21st Street
Colorado Springs, CO 80904
719-633-4080
American art pottery since 1899.

Jerome Venneman Pottery
658 - 66th Street
Oakland, CA 94609
510-653-5106

■ ■ *Wallpaper & Stencils*

Bradbury & Bradbury Art Wallpapers
P.O. Box 155
Benicia, CA 94510
707-746-1900
Handprinted art wallpapers.

Helen Foster Stencils
71 Main Street
Sanford, ME 04073
207-490-2625
*Reproduction and original Arts &
Crafts stencils.*

Carol Mead Wallpapers
434 Deerfield Road
Pomfret Center, CT 06259
860-963-1927
*Wallpapers and borders, including
C.F.A. Voysey patterns.*

Charles Rupert
2004 Oak Bay Avenue
Victoria, British Columbia V8R 1E4
William Morris wallpapers and fabrics.

Trimbelle River Studio & Design
Amy A. Miller
P.O. Box 568
Ellsworth, WI 54011
715-273-4844
Original Arts & Crafts stencil designs.

■ ■ *Rugs*

Blue Hills Studio
Nancy Thomas
400 Woodland Way
Greenville, SC 29607
864-232-4217
Custom-handcrafted wool rugs.

JAX Arts & Crafts Rugs
109 Parkway
Berea, KY 40403
606-986-5410

Nature's Loom
32 East 31st Street
New York, NY 10016
1-800-365-2002

■ ■ *Miscellaneous*

Mitchell Andrus
68 Central Avenue
Stirling, NJ 07980
908-647-7442
*Arts & Crafts furnishings and
accessories.*

Arroyo Craftsman
4509 LittleJohn Street
Baldwin Park, CA 91706
626-960-9411
*A wide selection of Arts & Crafts
lighting, from table lamps to
chandeliers.*

The Arts & Clay Co.
24 Pikes Lane
Woodstock, NY 12498
914-679-6875

J.R. Burrows and Company
P.O. Box 522
Rockland, MA 02370
1-800-347-1795

Fair Oak Workshops
P.O. Box 5578
River Forest, IL 60305
1-800-341-0597
*Quality Arts & Crafts furniture, textiles, rugs, dinnerware, copper
pieces, and stencils.*

Hammersmith Collection
P.O. Box 317
Buffalo, NY 14213
Roycroft mirrors.

Lunaform
P.O. Box 189
Sullivan, ME 04664
207-422-0923
*Hand-turned concrete reproductions
of Arts & Crafts garden pottery by
E. E. Soderholtz.*

Anita Munman
729 South Carpenter Avenue
Oak Park, IL 60304
708-383-2884
Arts & Crafts-period inspired art.

Omega Too
2204 San Pablo Avenue
Berkeley, CA 94702
510-843-3636
*Craftsman doors and architectural
elements, including gates, windows,
fixtures, lighting.*

United Crafts
127 West Putnam Avenue, Suite 123
Greenwich, CT 06830
203-869-4898
www.ucrafts.com
*Handcrafted accessories, including
textiles, pottery, and Jarvie-inspired
candlesticks.*

Kathleen West
P.O. Box 545
East Aurora, NY 14052
716-652-9125
kwestprintmaker@juno.com
*Limited-edition Arts & Crafts spoon-
printed, hand-colored block prints.*

■ **Galleries and Retail Sources**

Cathers & Dembrosky
43 East 10th Street
New York, NY 10003
212-353-1244

Circa 1910 Antiques
7206 Melrose Avenue
Los Angeles, CA 90046
213-965-1910

Craftsman Antiques
57-12 Telegraph Avenue
Oakland, CA 94609
510-595-7977

The Craftsman Home
3048 Claremont Avenue
Berkeley, CA 94705
510-655-6503

**The Craftsman's Guild and California
Heritage Gallery**
300 DeHaro Street
San Francisco, CA 94103
415-431-5425

Craftsman Style
1453 Fourth Street
Santa Monica, CA 90401
310-393-1468
*Period and contemporary Arts &
Crafts furnishings.*

Geoffrey Diner Gallery
1730 21st Street NW
Washington, DC 20009
202-483-5005

Fedde's
2350 East Colorado Boulevard
Pasadena, CA 91107
626-796-7103

Michael Fitzsimmons Decorative Arts
311 West Superior Street
Chicago, IL 60610
312-787-0496
*Arts & Crafts antiques and select
reproductions.*

Gallery 532
142 Duane Street
New York, NY 10013
212-219-1327
*Original and contemporary Arts &
Crafts furnishings.*

The Gamble House Bookstore
4 Westmoreland Place
Pasadena, CA 91103
626-449-4178
*Arts & Crafts books and decorative
and fine arts.*

Tim Gleason Gallery
77 Sullivan Street
New York, NY 10012
212-966-5777
*Specializing in Gustav Stickley
antiques but encompassing other makers of the period, including English
work; contemporary work includes
Gleason's own coffee table and club
chairs, and custom leather work.*

The Handwerk Shop
Portland, OR
503-236-7870
*Contemporary and original Arts &
Crafts furniture and accessories,
including Warren Hile furniture, Jim
Dailey clocks, and the shop's own line
of Morris chairs and Prairie settles.*

Historic Lighting
114 East Lemon Avenue
Monrovia, CA 91016
626-303-4899

Jeanne's Lamp & Mission Furniture
Liberty, MO
816-781-3206

The Joinery
Portland, OR
503-788-8547

Scott Jordan Furniture
New York, NY
212-620-4682

Lifetime Gallery
7111 Melrose Avenue
Los Angeles, CA 90046
213-939-7441

Isak Lindenauer Antiques
4143 19th Street
San Francisco, CA 94114
415-552-6436

The Mission Chair
Atlanta, GA
404-377-9239

Peter-Roberts Antiques, Inc.
134 Spring Street
New York, NY 10012
212-226-4777
*Arts & Crafts-period antiques, plus
some rugs, lamps, and furniture by
contemporary craftsmen.*

Thomas R. Reynolds Gallery
2291 Pine at Filmore
San Francisco, CA 94115
415-441-4093
*Fine art and select contemporary
craftsmanship in the Arts & Crafts
tradition.*

The Roycroft Shops
31 South Grove Street
East Aurora, NY 14052
716-655-0571
www.crafthome.com
More than 600 essentials for the craftsman home.

F. L. Wright Gallery
316 East Congress
Tucson, AZ 85701
520-622-3350
Period Mission furniture.

■ **Catalogs**

J. Peterman
1-800-231-7341
Clothing and furnishings company offering "Grove Park Chair" and other Arts & Crafts furniture.

Rejuvenation Lamp and Fixture Co.
1-800-526-7329
Period reproduction lighting fixtures.

Restoration Hardware
1-800-762-1005
Furnishings and fixtures company offering range of craftsman pieces.

Smith & Hawken
1-800-776-3336
Gardening catalog offering outdoor and indoor furniture.

Sundance
1-800-422-2770
Western clothing and Mission furniture.

Wood Classics
914-255-7871
Wood furniture, both assembled and in kit form.

■ **Architects and Interior Designers**

Mathew Bialecki
108 Main Street
New Paltz, NY 12561
Architects, interior designer, furniture designer in the Arts & Crafts tradition. (CK)?

The Cascade Joinery
1336 East Hemmi Road
Everson, WA 98247
360-398-8013
Timber-frame homes.

Karen L. Hovde
23 Oak Shore Court
Port Townsend, WA 98368
360-385-3161
"Interior vision in the Craftsman style."

J. Lohr Properties, Inc.
3215 Macomber Drive
Pebble Beach, CA 93953
408-626-1077
Builders specializing in craftsman-style homes.

Mimi London
8687 Melrose
Los Angeles, CA 90069
310-855-2567
Interior designer and furniture designer.

Gerald Lee Morosco Architects, P.C.
50 South 15th Street
Pittsburgh, PA 15203
412-431-4347

John F. Slaven, Architect
P.O. Box 3934
Visalia, CA 93278
209-627-4747
Specializing in new bungalows and restorations.

■ **Periodicals & Bookstores**

American Bungalow
123 South Baldwin Avenue
P.O. Box 756
Sierra Madre, CA 91025
818-355-1651

The Craftsman Homeowner Magazine
31 South Grove Street
East Aurora, NY 14052
716-652-3333

The Gamble House Bookstore
4 Westmoreland Place
Pasadena, CA 91103
626-449-4178, x 17

Old House Interiors
2 Main Street
Gloucester, MA 01930
1-800-462-0211

Old House Journal
2 Main Street
Gloucester, MA 01930
1-800-234-3797

Style 1900
333 North Main Street
Lambertville, NJ 08530
609-397-4104

The Tabby
The Arts & Crafts Press
P.O. Box 5217
Berkeley, CA 94705
510-849-2117

■ **Conferences, Tours & Lectures**

American Art Pottery Association Annual Convention
Linda Carrigan
P.O. Box 710
York Harbor, ME 03911
Three-day event featuring pottery show and sale, art pottery auction, and educational seminars.

Craftsman Farms
2352 Route 10W, Box 5
Morris Plains, NJ 07950
201-540-1165
Gustav Stickley's home, recently restored; lectures & tours. September symposium.

The Grove Park Inn Arts & Crafts Conference
290 Macon Avenue
Asheville, NC 28804
1-800-438-5800
Bruce Johnson, Conference Director:
704-254-1912
The largest, oldest Arts & Crafts show and sale in the country, held in February.

Historic Seattle Arts & Crafts Guild
605 First Avenue
Seattle, WA 98104
206-622-6952
Year-round tours, lectures and Arts & Crafts related activities.

Oak Park Visitors' Center
Oak Park, Illinois
708-848-1500
Guided walking tours of Frank Lloyd Wright-designed residences.

Pacific Northwest Arts & Crafts Show & Symposium
Historic Preservation League of Oregon
503-243-1923
Held annually in October.

Pasadena Heritage Craftsman Weekend
651 South St. John Avenue
Pasadena, CA 91105-2913
616-441-6333
Held annually in November.

Prairie Arts & Crafts Conference
Ed Walker
Milliken University
Decatur, IL 62522
217-424-6228
Held annually in September.

Study of the Arts & Crafts Movement at Roycroft
716-652-3333
Conferences, lectures, newsletter.

■ **Arts & Crafts Buildings & Displays Open to the Public**

Craftsman Farms
2352 Route 10W, Box 5
Morris Plains, NJ 07950
201-540-1165
Gustav Stickley's home, recently restored.

Frank Lloyd Wright Home & Studio
951 Chicago Avenue
Oak Park, IL 60302
708-848-1976
The architect and furniture designer's first self-designed home.

The Gamble House
4 Westmoreland Place
Pasadena, CA 91103
626-793-3334
Greene & Greene "ultimate bungalow."

The Hollyhock House
Barnesdale Art Park
4809 Hollywood Boulevard
Los Angeles, CA 213-662-7272
Frank Lloyd Wright textile-block house.

The Huntington Library
1151 Oxford Road
San Marino, CA 91108
626-405-2100
Permanent exhibit of Greene & Greene furniture designs.

Metropolitan Museum of Art
The Francis Little Living Room
1000 Fifth Avenue
New York, NY 10028
A reconstruction of a Frank Lloyd Wright room, complete with furniture and lighting.

Pleasant Home, The John Farson House
217 Home Avenue
Oak Park, IL 60302
708-383-2654
An 1897 house designed by Prairie-School architect George W. Maher.

Roycroft Inn
South Grove Street
East Aurora, NY 14052
716-652-5552
The original Roycroft Inn, recently restored.

Roycroft Museum
363 Oakwood Avenue
East Aurora, NY 14052
716-652-4735
Museum open to the public.

Swedenborgian Church
2107 Lyon Street
San Francisco, CA 94115
Landmark Bernard Maybeck-designed church.

Thorsen House
2307 Piedmont Avenue
Berkeley, CA 92704
510-540-9157
Greene & Greene-designed house.